The Single Market and Tomorrow's Europe

A Progress Report from the European Commission

Research on the *Single Market Review*
funded by the European Commission

Presented by
Mario MONTI   Member of the European Commission

This book summarizes the progress of the single market to date and
provides an essential key to the review of the single market
undertaken by the European Commission. The findings of the *Single
Market Review* have been published as a series of 38 reports and 1
Business survey containing detailed information on specific industry
sectors (for list of titles, see pp 159–61 of Appendix C).

Written by David Buchan

The Single Market and Tomorrow's Europe

A Progress Report from the European Commission

presented by

Mario MONTI

Office for Official Publications of the European Communities

Kogan Page Publishers

British Library Cataloguing in Publication Data
A CIP record for this book is available from the British Library.

First published in 1996

Typeset by Northern Phototypesetting Co Ltd, Bolton
Printed in England by Clays Ltd, St Ives plc

© European Communities, 1996

Office for Official Publications of the European Communities
2 rue Mercier, I.-2985 Luxembourg
ISBN 92-827-8701-X   Catalogue number: C1-01-96-010-EN-C

Kogan Page
120 Pentonville Road, London N1 9JN
ISBN 0 7494 2266 1

Contents

List of tables			vi
List of figures			viii
Foreword			ix

Chapter	**1**	A Flying Start	1
Chapter	**2**	Putting the Machine in Motion	7
Chapter	**3**	The Broadest Barriers – Breached, if not Broken	13
Chapter	**4**	Milestones in Manufacturing	41
Chapter	**5**	Breaking New Ground in Services	59
Chapter	**6**	The 'New Look' Market	77
Chapter	**7**	Competition and Competitiveness	95
Chapter	**8**	Growth, Jobs and Cohesion	105
Chapter	**9**	Protecting People and the Environment	115
Chapter	**10**	Networks beyond the Nineties	125
Chapter	**11**	Looking to the Future	135

Appendix A.	The Structure of the Research	146
Appendix B.	Results of Eurostat Business Survey	149
Appendix C.	The Single Market Review Series	159

List of tables

2.1   State of implementation of Directives concerning
the Internal Market   11

3.1   Impact of single market measures aimed at removing
technical barriers   24

3.2   Supplier response and public sector import penetration   36

4.1   Impact of the single market   42

4.2   Estimated EU equipment price premiums, 1985-95   45

4.3   'Have these directives contributed to the following?'   54

4.4   Imports of finished medicines from other EU member
nations as a percentage of consumption (1988-94)   56

5.1   Effectiveness of single market measures in removing
barriers to the free provision of services (as perceived by
economic operators)   61

5.2   Cecchini Report results: the prices of five products
in 1987   65

5.3   Postal survey study results: the prices of five products
in 1996   65

5.4   Cultural factors preventing advertising standardisation
for advertising agencies   73

5.5   Cultural factors preventing advertising standardisation
for companies   73

6.1   Share of intra-EU trade in total trade: manufacturing   81

6.2   Share of intra-EU trade in total trade: services   82

6.3   Evolution of concentration at EU level   89

6.4   Changes in size and concentration by industry type   91

6.5 Coefficients of price variation for selected groupings   92
7.1 Change in competition level on the domestic market in
    recent years   96
7.2 Impact of the single market programme on enterprises'
    unit costs by size: manufacturing sector   99
7.3 Importance of the single market programme to the
    development of the strategy of enterprises in recent years:
    manufacturing sector   100
7.4 Importance of the single market programme to the
    development of the strategy of enterprises in recent years:
    service sector   100
8.1 Gross value added per capita growth rates after 1987
    compared with 1975-87 trend   107
8.2 Significance of the EU's FDI inflows to GDP by Member
    State (1986-93)   111
10.1 Annual EU-wide telecom sector projections   128
10.2 Ranking of overall benefits of each scenario as compared
    with the 2005 Base   132

List of figures

3.1	Winners and losers: despatches	17
3.2	Winners and losers: acquisitions	18
3.3	System preferences	20
3.4	Making the mutual recognition principle work	27
3.5	Functioning of the 'new approach' to technical harmonisation	31
4.1	Chemical industry capital spending on environmental protection	51
4.2	Intra-EC exports as a percentage of total exports, 1993	51
4.3	Intra-EC imports as a percentage of total imports, 1993	52
5.1	Change in loan prices by country and impact of the single market programme	63
5.2	Change in deposit prices by country and impact of the single market programme	64
5.3	EUR-8 averages: price of demand and time deposits	64
6.1	Single market - the Virtuous Circle	78
6.2	Share of intra-EU imports in total imports for EUR-15: trade in goods	83
6.3	Cross-border mergers and acquisitions where a Community firm is the target	87
6.4	Evolution of Europe's three leading suppliers	90
7.1	Price-cost margins, 1980-92	97

Foreword

The Single Market – A new commitment

Mario Monti, European Commissioner responsible for the Single Market

The Single Market is at the core of the European Union. Its creation was one of the main objectives of the original Rome Treaty. The eight-year programme to complete it between 1985 and 1992 was the most ambitious target that the European Community ever set itself. The fact that the target was in a large measure reached is one of the Community's enduring successes.

The Single Market remains at the centre of the European Union's concerns today. Opening up fifteen national markets into one Single Market, ensuring open competition and preparing for its enlargement to many other countries may well be regarded as the greatest 'supply side' exercise ever in world economics – a huge exercise to stimulate production, increase competition, reduce prices and thus increase demand. The completion of the Single Market and its good state of health will be a major contributor to the achievement of the Union's current and future political objectives.

First and foremost, there is increasing recognition on the part of governments, business and employees of the important link between the Single Market, economic growth and fuller employment. Only a properly working market, through full international economic integration, will stimulate the competition, restructuring and innovation which can provide lasting employment in Europe.

Second, cohesion between regions is increasing as the Single Market provides opportunities in the form of increased trade and investment for the development of new skills and technologies in all parts of the Union. The countries which are 'catching up' benefit from new levels of efficiency and productivity. The countries which did not have so far to go also benefit from better trade and investment opportunities with other Member States.

Third, in the run-up to Economic and Monetary Union, an effective Single Market is able to guarantee the economic stability necessary to underpin the move to a Single Currency. The Single Currency will also reduce the cost to business and consumers of managing different currencies and help markets to work more efficiently by revealing price differences right across the Union.

Fourth, the enlargement of the Union and the successful preparation of associated countries for their participation in the Single Market presents a major challenge, but meeting it will determine the conditions under which enlargement takes place. The Single Market also helps associated countries with the difficult task of approximating their laws and getting into step with the practical application of the rules.

At the end of the eight-year legislative programme which preceded the entry into force of the Single Market in December 1992, the Council of Ministers asked the Commission to present in the course of 1996, an analysis of the impact and effectiveness of the legislation which had been put into place.

The Commission began work on this task over two years ago. Extensive background research was organized, comprising thirty-eight independent studies of various sections of the economy, areas of legislation or economic variables, together with a large scale survey of EU businesses. I have been privileged to lead this major research programme, with the help of my colleagues, and to steer it to its conclusions. Indeed, the results of this work formed the basis of a political report presented by the Commission in November 1996.[1]

For the first time in the short life of the Single Market, we now have empirically derived evidence of how we are doing. Now we can see; we can begin to walk by sight, rather than only by faith. This means that we can use this valuable information to start to 'fine tune' the Single Market in terms of what needs to be done, and who needs to do it.

All of the background research, about 10,000 pages in all, will be published by the Commission and will, no doubt, attract attention from the specialists most directly concerned. But I felt that it was necessary that the Commission try to reach a wider audience on a subject which is of direct relevance to businesses and to individual citizens. Hence the decision to produce this book, which is intended to tell the story of the successes of the Single Market so far, to those who are directly affected by it. It also aims to highlight areas where we need to do more, for example, to complete the work on the free movement of persons, company law and taxation, and to address future challenges such as the Information Society.

What follows is a colourful but accurate account of what the Community has been trying to achieve, how far it has succeeded and (occasionally) failed and, above all, what difference the Single Market is making in terms of presenting new opportunities for prosperity to our businesses and citizens.

Clearly, the story does not end here. The Single Market is not an isolated event which happened in January 1993 but a continual process. It is not so much a legal framework as an attitude of mind. We cannot afford to be complacent. There is still plenty of work to be done before we have reached our ultimate goal, which is to make the Single Market operate with full efficiency.

In its Report, the Commission set out its priorities for the Single Market agenda. Its message is simple: the Single Market is already yielding significant benefits but it will yield more if we can successfully overcome remaining problems.

In the first place, Member States must renew their commitment to the Single Market. They must start by delivering on their existing commitments, in particular by implementing and vigorously enforcing Community legislation and Treaty principles. Second, we must attack the tendency to over-regulate and impose unnecessary burdens on businesses and our economy, at both Community and national level. Third, we must have the political courage to take the decisions necessary to

---

[1] Communication from the Commission to the European Parliament and the Council on the 'Impact and effectiveness of the Single Market', COM (96) 520 final of 30 October 1996 (Cat. No. CB-CO-96-558-EN-C), Office for Official Publications of the European Communities.

remove the remaining obstacles to an effective Single Market, even if this appears to touch on such sensitive areas as taxation or border controls on people. Finally, we must use all the instruments available under other Community policies to help the Single Market work better.

I have one last message which also is echoed in this book. It is that in the final analysis markets are made by businesses and their customers, not by governments. The Community has come a long way since 1985 and has, by and large, delivered a single legal framework in which businesses can operate freely, and customers can choose freely, across frontiers. But the Single Market is much more than an economic enterprise. Together with other Community policies it has contributed tangible benefits to citizens of the Union: lower prices and more consumer choice, the extension of personal freedom and rights, higher living standards, better health and safety at work, product safety and reliability, and a safer environment. We can and should do more. But further refinement of Community Single Market legislation cannot substitute for the energy and dynamism of entrepreneurs to compete for business in new markets. It is on this that our future prosperity depends. The other important market players are the customers. Individual consumers, as well as companies, need to be better informed about the possibilities now open to them so that they can stimulate ever-higher standards of economic performance. I hope that this book will go some way towards helping to achieve that aim.

Chapter 1

A Flying Start

The European Union's single market is in a state of constant evolution and extension. Created to open up national economies, thereby increasing growth, competitiveness and living standards in Europe, the single market has become the largest and most complete free trade area in the world, inhabited by 370m people who between them generate output of Ecus 6,441bn.

It now extends beyond the EU's 15 members, to embrace Norway, Iceland and Liechtenstein, and early in the next century it will stretch into eastern Europe as countries there join the EU. It is also subject to adaptation as EU decision-makers, national governments and business respond to economic, technological and social change inside this enormous marketplace by amending, refining and simplifying old rules and coming up with new ones. The single market programme has thus become a process of dynamic change, rather than something static and set in concrete.

But the main legislative architecture of the single market was built in the late 1980s and the first half of the 1990s, as most of the 282 Directives and proposals set out in the European Commission's '1992' blueprint were laid, stone by stone, in place. Between 1985 and 1992, an unprecedented volume of legislation was adopted. The change to qualified majority voting and the willingness of Member States to compromise meant that nearly all the key measures were adopted before the target date of 31 December 1992. Many of the cracks were filled in with scores more pieces of implementing legislation. Some of the legislation is only just coming into force, because of transitional periods or special derogations for certain member states. But it is now possible to take a general look at whether the hopes and fears aroused by the single market programme are beginning to happen.

That is the aim of this book. It is based on a big new research effort. To help find out what has happened and to plan for the single market's future, the European Commission asked independent experts from around the Union to conduct a series of 38 in-depth studies and itself coordinated a business survey (see Appendix A). Some of these studies take an across the board look at such features as trade, investment and competition patterns. Others delve deep into sectors like cars and pharmaceuticals. In volume terms, this is twice the amount of research that went into the famous Cecchini Report of 1988 – The single market's potential. Rightly so. For the task of establishing what *has* happened, as distinct from what *should* happen, is doubly difficult. It requires an effort to winnow out all the other factors affecting Europe in recent years – like globalisation of the world economy, technology shifts, Germany's reunification in 1990, the 1992-93 disruptions among European currencies, and an attempt to isolate the 'single market effect' on the EU's economy.

The research shows that, so far, the single market programme appears, among other things, to have:

- increased output in the EU by more than 1 per cent, with more positive results to come;
- raised the level of employment by between 300,000 and 900,000 more jobs than there would otherwise have been;
- produced inflation rates 1.0 to 1.5 per cent lower than they would be without the single market;
- stimulated investment in the EU by an additional 2.7 per cent;
- attracted extra foreign direct investment to the European Union (44 per cent of world FDI inflows in the early 1990s, compared to 28.2 per cent between 1982 and 1987);
- allowed poorer EU states to grow faster than the richer ones;
- intensified intra-EU trade, with the share of manufactured goods and services which EU states export to each other increasing by, respectively, 14 and 7.6 percentage points over the past decade;
- almost doubled the share of public sector purchases from other member states from 6 to 10 per cent;

- knocked more than Ecus 5bn a year off the costs of Europe's traders and road hauliers because they no longer have to stop at internal EU borders for routine customs and fiscal checks;
- accelerated price reductions in telecommunications equipment by 7 per cent, saving buyers up to Ecus 1.5-2bn a year;
- kept air transport traffic 20 per cent higher than it otherwise would have been during the early 1990s recession.

But the single market programme has proved disappointing in that:

- it has so far benefited small and medium-sized companies less than larger groups which had the structures to exploit the new market better;
- it has taken longer to implement than originally anticipated and the full effects in terms of competitiveness for European business have yet to be realised.

These are, however, just the starker shades emerging from a complex picture. It is clear that neither the best hopes nor worst fears surrounding the single market programme have been realised. There were strong hopes that the programme would set Europe on a higher, and possibly permanently higher, growth path. Removal of trade barriers would create more competition, drive down prices and costs, thereby stimulating demand from consumers and encouraging companies to make further efficiency-related investments to gain economies of scale – and so on in a beneficial chain reaction. The world-wide economic recession of the early 1990s put paid to early realisation of that hope, and with it the prospect of a big increase in job creation.

Yet, the EU did pick itself up and perform better in the late 1980s and the early 1990s than either the US or Japan in relation to their respective growth trends of previous years. The single market programme has gradually delivered more competition. This did not prevent unemployment rates from rising in Europe. The single market programme undoubtedly speeded up restructuring in some sectors, which had hitherto been shielded by multiple barriers. But liberalisation benefited other sectors like telecom and information services, which are proving to be major net providers of the jobs of the future.

The single market also provoked trepidation among poorer EU member states that they might suffer in a more competitive market and lose ground to the industries of richer member states. The evidence is that neither happened, except perhaps in the case of Greece. Spain, Portugal and Ireland grew faster than the EU average. Much of this was, of course, due to increased EU structural funding which these countries received and which they spent mainly on infrastructure. But if the single market did bring with it some increased specialisation – and it did – this did not lead to poorer member states being generally shut out of newer, higher technology industries into which they had begun to venture.

'Fortress Europe' has proved a myth, too. At the outset of the single market programme, many in Washington and Tokyo accused the EU of trying to shut them out of the emerging single market. In support of their case, they cited EU provisions for reciprocity in financial services, limits on Japanese car shipments and a non-binding quota aimed at US films. As it has turned out, the EU has never used the reciprocity provision in financial services; Japanese firms are now largely supplying the EU with cars made in Europe rather than shipped from Japan; and Hollywood has found a non-binding quota no bar to its exports to Europe. Imports from major competitors like the US and Japan did increase, but less than the job-creating investment coming in from those two countries. And, from the European viewpoint, such import competition has provided a useful downward pressure on prices, which otherwise proved rather impervious to the effects of the single market. The single market programme coincided with the Uruguay Round of the GATT trade negotiations, and in some ways, set the agenda for those negotiations. The EU thereby proved itself a building block, and not a stumbling block, for an open international trading order.

The single market programme gave rise, too, to voices prophesying that, despite the lighter approach towards harmonisation, there would be an increasingly bland uniformity of products on offer to Europe's consumers, as Europe's companies took advantage of the disappearance of customs, technical and regulatory barriers to develop 'single products for the single market'. In fact, far from being suppressed, consumer choice has increased hugely. This phenomenon is partly related to information technology allowing manufacturers to make multiple variants of their products and to the logistics revolution – itself a direct result of removing border controls and liberalising road transport – permitting speedy dispatch of these products to Europe's varied markets.

Access to those markets is now far easier. The market for industrial goods is now highly integrated within the EU, due to single market legislation that built on earlier achievements. The single market programme's assault on barriers to the provision of cross-border services was, by contrast, far more radical because of the many national rules and regulations surrounding services. Progress in creating pan-European markets for services is thus inevitably slower, but it has produced greater competition in services with consumers seeing the benefit in terms of wider choice.

In general, however, examples of where the single market programme is clearly *seen* as the driving force for change in a particular sector are comparatively rare. The predominant picture that emerges from the independent studies and from the 13,500 companies which responded to a Eurostat survey (see Appendix B) is that the EU measures have been as much an *enabler*, as a *driver*, of change.

That is to say, the single market has helped to create an environment where businesses are more likely to pursue pan-European strategies and to enter another market in the EU, even though managers may not see it as the main reason for the strategic decisions they have taken. The EU seems to have performed this enabling role in air transport, satellite broadcasting, corporate banking, car manufacture, telecommunications and mobile telephony. In all these areas, market access has become freer, and the level of cross-border competition, sales and mergers has increased.

By contrast, much of Europe's retail banking and insurance, pharmaceutical and energy industries remain structured along national lines. This reflects the fact that initial competition from outside prompted them to target their domestic market. This may be a 'stepping stone' to gearing up for competitive cross-border activity. There is also the preference that most individual Europeans still have for financial service companies of their own nationality or at least based within their own country, and the control that national governments have exercised, in the name of medical safety and energy security, over their drugs and energy industries.

The existence of these controls, and the possibility of relaxing some of them, means that there are still big potential gains to be squeezed out of the single market. To try to gauge the size of these gains, the Commission asked independent experts to examine the effect of further liberalisation in three areas – energy, telecoms/information services and transport. Chapter 10 contains the full results, but the bottom line of the studies is that:

- electricity liberalisation, to the extent agreed in summer 1996, will produce savings of Ecus 4–6bn a year for electricity users by 2005;
- full liberalisation of telecommunications, which is already underway, combined with diffusion of information technology and unchecked expansion of information services, would produce an accumulating increase in overall output amounting to more than 1 per cent of GDP by 2005;
- completion of the Trans-European transport Networks (TENs) already proposed by the Commission, combined with major improvements to railways and pricing changes affecting all forms of transport, could yield total potential savings to Europe's transport users of more than Ecus 130bn a year, or 1-1.5 per cent of the Union's GDP, by 2005.

Prizes of this magnitude are clearly worth aiming at.

Chapter 2

Putting the Machine in Motion

The single market is not only a mass market, but creating it has also become a mass endeavour. What might have seemed an elitist blueprint at the outset is steadily involving more people – not only the European Commission, governments of the member states and the European Parliament, but also national parliamentarians, trade associations, standard-setters, companies, judges, consumers and citizens. Their involvement is vital if the rights and freedoms offered by the single market are to be taken up and used.

The origin of the single market programme is well known. By the mid-1980s it began to dawn on many that, after nearly 30 years, the European Community still had no real common market, that many of the freedoms prescribed in the Treaty of Rome for capital, goods, services and people remained a dead letter, and that removing this economic fragmentation and these legal failings might pull Europe out of its doldrums and help it compete better with North Americans and East Asians. So the Commission produced its 1985 White Paper of 282 proposals to give the Treaty freedoms some real meaning at last.

Within the year, the member states made their major contribution by calling their first inter-governmental conference since 1957 and by signing the Single European Act. The key feature of this was to extend majority voting to almost every issue at stake in the single market, with the important exception of tax where the rule of unanimity still holds. The result was a burst of European legislation, with the Commission churning out the White Paper proposals in the form of Directives and regulations, for debate and approval by the Council of Ministers and the

European Parliament. The Commission set a date, 1 January 1993, for 'completion' of its single market programme. This date was intended as a spur to EU legislators, certainly not as marking an end to their efforts. In fact, it roughly marked the point where most of the legislation needed for the single market had been passed. By 1995, the Commission was producing one third of its level of draft legislation five years earlier (19 draft proposals compared to 61 in 1990).

But the story does not end there. As the spate of new laws has slackened, so the task of ensuring they are obeyed becomes more important. A few dozen of the original White Paper proposals took the form of regulations, which once passed by the Council of Ministers in Brussels and the European Parliament in Strasbourg enter directly and automatically into force in member states. Most of the measures – no less than 221 – took the form of Directives, which needed to be converted, or 'transposed' in the EU jargon, into national law by national parliaments. Not all have been. By October 1996, an average of 91 per cent of all of the internal market Directives, including the implementing legislation, was on member states' statute books, with Denmark holding the best record of 97.8 per cent, and the newest member states of Sweden, Austria and Finland bringing up the rear with transposition rates of less than 88 per cent. The spotlight has tended to focus on the fate of the legislation stemming from the original White Paper. But there is a mass of secondary, implementing legislation – some of it in the form of Directives – that also requires action by national parliaments and civil services.

Governments drag their feet for various reasons. Sometimes, a new government is reluctant to put into law an EU measure which its predecessor agreed or was prepared to accept. More often, it succumbs to pressures from domestic industries who urge it to delay the transposition of EU legislation in order to keep their sectors protected for just a little bit longer.

A particular instance of this lies in insurance in Germany, where specialised health insurance companies continue to be protected from rivals offering several types of insurance, despite a specific requirement in the Third Non-Life Insurance Directive that all insurance companies must be allowed to offer health cover. A general example occurs in public procurement. Several governments have been slow to put into their national law the new rules on opening up public contracts to competitive cross-border bidding (see Chapter 3). In fact, only three member states have fulfilled their obligation to transpose the eleven public procurement Directives effectively. The habit of governments to reserve their juiciest contracts for domestic companies, 'the home team', is proving hard to break. It is a classic illustration of how governments, and companies, want to have their cake and eat it, happy to seize on opportunities in neighbouring markets but still keen to keep their own market off-limits to competitors.

In some instances, the necessary legislation ends up on national statute books, but in a different form. This is because while some member states faithfully copy EU-agreed language into their national law, others like to re-organise and re-phrase it. This carries the risk, even perhaps the aim, of elaborating on the requirements in the EU measures in such a way as to discriminate against foreigners.

The job of chasing up member states which have failed to adopt EU directives, or adopt them correctly or to implement them fully, falls to the Commission. Its weapons are political pressure and/or legal action. This involves public reminders to member states of their failure to live up in practice to their commitment to the single market, warning letters and eventually law suits brought in the European Court of Justice. Single market legislation is firmly grounded in the EU Treaty. A key doctrine of the single market programme – the requirement that member states mutually recognise each other's industrial and commercial rules and therefore accept each other's goods and services – actually stems from an earlier European Court ruling. In addition, the 1992 Maastricht Treaty allows the European Court to fine a member state that flouts one of its rulings.

As a result, just the threat of European Court action is often sufficient to bring a member state into line. This was how the Commission managed to settle recent problems involving, for example, pesticide and pharmaceutical imports into Germany, railway contracts, beer and food imports into Italy, sporting gun ammunition imports into France, and discriminatory regional schemes and fruit juice imports into Greece.

The Commission makes public what it believes are infringements of the single market, not only to try to shame the offending member state into remedying the problem, but also to alert the public to its rights under EU law. It encourages companies and individuals to take action in national courts if they feel they have suffered as a result of single market rules not being applied. Community law is directly applicable and, unlike the European Court, national courts can grant injunctions to suspend offending measures and award damages payments.

Legal action is often too costly or time-consuming to be an option for a private individual or a small company. It also goes against the grain for companies to police their own customers – which, in the area of public procurement, are governments themselves. Nevertheless, in a market of 370m people, the Commission has to rely on its elected representatives in the European Parliament and on consumer and industry organisations to be its eyes and ears in the member states and to alert it to infringements of single market law. Naturally, this presupposes that companies, consumers and citizens know what their rights are. To improve such knowledge and to encourage 'grass roots' enforcement of single market law, the Commission is planning a major information campaign, 'Citizens First'!

In terms of shaping the single market rules, there is an increasingly wide cast of players involved. Prominent among them are the new European standards bodies. The EU has delegated to them the vital job of drawing up new European norms to replace the old national technical barriers, removed by single market legislation. Business, too, has an important role to play in shaping new legislation. National employers' organisations and those such as UNICE, the Union of Industrial and Employers' Confederations of Europe, have carried out their own surveys and studies and come up with suggested improvements to the regulatory process and possible reductions to burdensome and costly over-regulation.

Much of the original White Paper was relatively easy to draft. Some of it was just amendments to fill in the holes in old legislation, for example, in public procurement. But the EU is facing new and more complex issues like those raised by advances in information technology and biotechnology. Regulation here requires even more careful preparation. To this end, the Commission is tending towards the publication of preliminary 'Green' papers for discussion with trade/industry associations before coming up with any legislative proposal.

There is economic as well as political logic behind this effort to get the widest possible acceptance and enforcement of single market rules.

	Measures notified	Not applicable	Derogations	Measures not notified	Partial notification	Infringement for non-conformity
		(1410 Directives in force) **Breakdown of Situation by Member State** (24 October 1996)				
DK	1238	141	0	25	3	3
NL	1236	133	0	28	7	6
UK	1196	140	0	45	18	11
E	1218	104	1	62	10	15
L	1178	134	0	88	4	6
IRL	1164	140	0	89	7	10
F	1156	127	0	101	9	17
D	1154	129	0	99	11	17
P	1197	79	3	108	6	17
EL	1163	109	3	125	1	9
I	1141	128	0	116	5	20
B	1148	117	0	123	14	8
S	1167	47	23	137	35	1
A	1107	52	52	168	30	1
FIN	1005	118	6	144	136	1

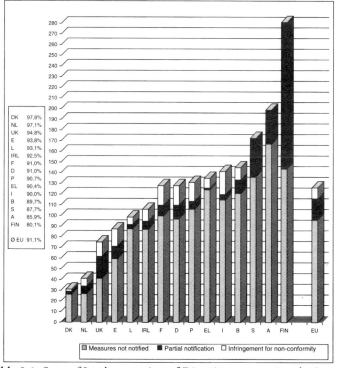

DK	97,8%
NL	97,1%
UK	94,8%
E	93,8%
L	93,1%
IRL	92,5%
F	91,0%
D	91,0%
P	90,7%
EL	90,4%
I	90,0%
B	89,7%
S	87,7%
A	85,9%
FIN	80,1%
Ø EU	91,1%

☒ Measures not notified ■ Partial notification ☐ Infringement for non-conformity

Table 2.1 State of Implementation of Directives concerning the Internal Market

Companies need the assurance of fair competition before they enter foreign markets. If they feel the game there is rigged in favour of a 'home team' which somehow plays under different rules or which can commit fouls without the referee noticing or imposing penalties, they will prefer to remain in their national league, rather than compete in the European Championship.

Table 2.1 shows clearly which teams are in the 'First Division' and which are in the lower divisions when it comes to implementing single market legislation.

Chapter 3

The Broadest Barriers – Breached, if not Broken

The broadest barriers have been, as one might expect, those maintained by governments themselves. And it is a tribute to the belated common sense of European governments that they did allow a frontal assault on these economic barricades to be made, even if on the side they have sometimes tried since to guard their own national preserves, particularly, of course, in public procurement.

Within the Union, these barriers fall, or fell, into three categories:

- the multiple checks to which customs officials subjected all goods at internal EU borders. These controls were, of course, not in order to exact tariffs; intra-EU trade had been free of tariffs since the late 1960s – but for the purpose of administering Value Added Tax, of carrying out health, veterinary and national security checks on goods crossing borders and of collecting trade statistics;
- the technical barriers imposed by states on goods being sold in their territory. Such barriers caused companies a big headache, requiring the reconfiguring, relabelling and repackaging of products for different national markets, the registration of certain goods like cars or pharmaceuticals with national authorities, and the constant retesting of products to comply with local health and safety rules;
- the peculiar propensity of governments not necessarily to seek out the best bargains regardless of origin, but rather to reserve orders for their own companies for political reasons or as a short-sighted form of industrial policy.

REMOVING CUSTOMS AND TAX CONTROLS AT BORDERS

Travellers within the European Union may still occasionally experience some delay at the Union's internal borders, if immigration officers or frontier police choose to examine their passports, or customs officers make a spot check for drugs or some other controlled substance.

But routine frontier controls on goods have gone. The chronic queues of trucks at internal EU border crossing points have disappeared since the start of 1993. Europe's traders and road hauliers now have a clear run through internal EU borders, saving them time and money. This has in turn produced new patterns of pan-European distribution, run by a new breed of logistics companies. This ability to move goods across internal EU frontiers without delay is now quite taken for granted.

Before 1993, every truckload of goods had to stop at internal EU borders for customs and tax clearance, and sometimes for inspection. Even where goods had already been cleared for export before arriving at the border, or were to be cleared for import beyond the frontier, documents had to be checked. Trucks carrying goods for simple transit across the EU had to have their documents and seals on their cargo checked. Clearing customs at these border points also involved accounting for VAT and, in the case of alcohol, tobacco and fuel, for excise. To deal with all this, most traders engaged freight forwarders, who themselves often hired customs agents, though this work was slightly less onerous in some northern European countries which implemented simpler procedures.

On 1 January 1993, customs checks at internal EU borders on goods for export, import and transit across the EU were simply abolished. This saved 60 million customs forms per year and some 85 per cent of 'red tape' in transit procedures. Instead a new system was introduced to account for taxes and to provide trade statistics. Back at their headquarters, companies now use their regular VAT returns to account for VAT on the goods they have traded, though their national authorities periodically verify this information by asking them for a list of their suppliers and customers in other EU states. Trade statistics are no longer collected at internal EU frontiers, but are reported by companies to a new system called INTRASTAT.

Not surprisingly, of all the single market programme's many measures, the abolition of customs and fiscal frontier formalities within the EU is the most visible and the most widely acclaimed. Some 62 per cent of the 13,500 companies responding to a Eurostat survey said they benefited from the end to border delays. And this benefit is quantifiable.

Abolition of routine borders controls on goods has reduced costs for Europe's traders and road hauliers by more than Ecus 5bn a year.[1] This saving is the equivalent of about 0.7 per cent of the EU's total trade turnover. Before 1993, the cost of complying with all the customs red tape at internal frontiers is estimated to have cost traders around Ecus 7.5bn a year, based on 1992 travel levels but expressed in today's money, while the cost of complying with the current system is put at Ecus 2.3bn a year according to the Customs & frontiers study. A saving of two thirds of one per cent may not seem large and something like total trade is rather abstract to most people. But if applied to a measure like net margin (profit before tax and interest) which has concrete meaning for businesses the saving becomes more significant. If, for example, a company achieves a net margin of 10 per cent of its turnover, then a saving which represents 0.66 per cent of its turnover would boost its net margin by nearly 7 per cent. Considered this way, small figures begin to look interesting.

But the new system of VAT accounting and statistics collection still imposes a cost on companies of roughly Ecus 2.3bn a year. This figure does not include the costs of carrying out transactions in member states where the trader is not established. Such transactions are estimated to be five or six time more expensive to traders than domestic ones because they are obliged to use tax representatives. In addition, companies had to bear a one-off cost of adapting to the new system in 1993. Generally, this involved companies and traders doing in-house what they had previously contracted out to agents. This brought managers face to face with administrative inconveniences of which they had no previous direct experience, and with administrative costs that had been previously considered as transport charges and loaded on to the customer or absorbed in the cost of sales. In many companies, overworked finance departments found themselves having to make INTRASTAT as well as VAT reports, while shipping departments that had traditionally dealt with trade statistics were often disbanded or downsized. For most companies, the cost, in terms of hiring new staff or buying new computer software, did not exceed Ecus 15,000, but for about a third of traders the expense of adapting to the new regime seems to have been above Ecus 25,000.

However, the savings are considerable, falling mostly into a band of Ecus 10–30 per consignment, but a substantial number of traders in Italy, Spain, Germany and the Netherlands report savings of up to or over Ecus 100 per consignment. In the case of Italy and Spain, this is due to the high level of customs agency fees that prevailed there before 1993. In the case of Germany and the Netherlands, the higher savings are reported by those companies that before 1993 happened to have their own in-house customs departments which have now been reduced or disbanded. German cross-border trade appears to have benefited from the highest aggregate savings, partly because of the sheer high volume of trade involved.

In general terms, traders in Mediterranean countries have seen the biggest improvement, while the smallest improvement came in Denmark because of the low cost and high efficiency of its previous system. The biggest aggregate savings have come in those states with the largest intra-EU trade volume and those with the highest costs. Thus, the biggest beneficiaries appear to be Germany, at least in volume terms, Italy and Spain, and the smallest Denmark, Luxembourg and Ireland, with the remainder in between.

The speed with which trading companies have recouped what they spent on switching to the new trade and tax reporting system has varied according to the amount of money they are saving from not having to pay agent fees and from not having their trucks tied up at borders, as well as according to the volume of their cross-border shipments. For some companies, particularly the big traders, the payback was quick. Companies representing about one third of intra-EU trade (by number of individual consignments) report that they recouped the switch-over costs within the first quarter of 1993. The proportion of companies claiming a payback rose to 50 per cent by the end of 1993. Four years later there are still 20 per cent of traders who claim not to have recouped the cost of the new system. Nonetheless, the ratio of winners to losers appears to be somewhere between 6:1 and 7:1. Figures 3.1 and 3.2 show the numbers of winners and losers per country in relation to despatches

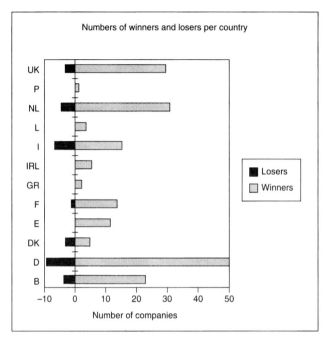

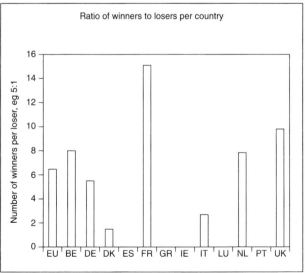

Figure 3.1 Winners and losers: despatches

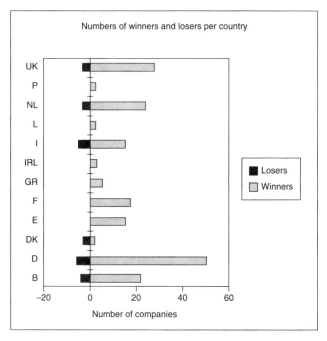

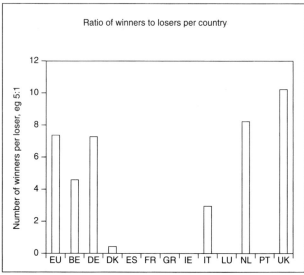

Figure 3.2 Winners and losers: acquisitions

and 'acquisitions' (or receipts) of goods shipped between the member states.

However, in spite of the strong predominance of winners over losers from the present system, most companies are not content with the current transitional system for VAT. This requires complex arrangements so that goods can be exported zero-rated on VAT, without fraud, so that the tax is collected in the 'consuming' country. About half of EU companies, particularly in Germany – despite the global score of German cross-border trade, individual German traders did not necessarily benefit more than those in other member states – and the UK, evidently hanker after the relative simplicity of the old pre-1993 system on VAT, though, broadly speaking, most firms in southern European countries as well as in France and Belgium are content with the new status quo.

But, given the choice by their governments, over two-thirds of all companies say they are ready to move on to the even greater simplicity of the definitive VAT system proposed by the Commission. Under this system VAT would be paid in the country where the goods in question were bought, just as in domestic trade. There is a substantial majority for moving on to this system in France, Germany, Spain and Italy, with a similar majority in all other countries except for Luxembourg and Ireland where the sample size of companies interviewed was too small to draw general conclusions. Figure 3.3 shows the comparison between preferences between the pre-1993 arrangement and the present system (the upper box) and between an origin based system and the present one.

Road hauliers should be the most direct beneficiaries of an end to chronic border delays. And before 1993 these delays were chronic, generally bad in southern Europe and especially so on the borders between Spain/Portugal, Greece/Italy, Spain/France and Italy/France. The tailbacks of trucks have by no means disappeared since. Today's worst delays are reported at the Franco-Spanish border and at Austria's borders with Germany and Italy. The entry into the EU of Austria, which by its accession treaty is allowed to enforce environmental limits on trucks crossing its territory, has done nothing to ease trade between Germany and Italy.

But the ending of old-style frontier delays is estimated to have created a *potential* gross saving of around Ecus 800m a year to the road haulage

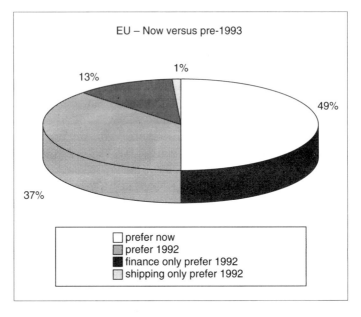

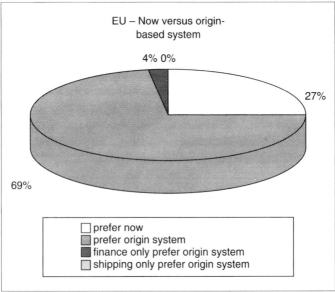

Figure 3.3 System preferences

industry.[2] The cost of today's residual delays is put at around Ecus 55m a year, mainly accounted for by average waiting times of around one hour at Austrian borders and of some 40 minutes at most crossing points between Spain and France. But, of course, the *real* saving to hauliers depends on how much of the time 'saved' can now be spent driving. Not only are truck drivers now subject to much tighter health and safety controls, such as maximum driving and minimum rest periods, but many of them had grown accustomed to taking their meal and rest breaks at frontier points which often developed into truck-stops. And many clearly intend to go on doing so.

As one driver told a Commission consultant, 'the only thing that has changed is that I don't have to keep looking out of the cafe window to check whether the customs queue has moved on'. Depending on what assumptions are made about average loads, and therefore about the frequency of vehicle movements, the real saving to the haulage industry from the reduction in frontier delays is put at around Ecus 370m a year, or at least somewhere in the range of Ecus 275m-450m.

Have road hauliers passed these cost savings on to their customers in the form of lower freight rates? Generally, it seems not but perhaps they were not able to. For road freight, increased excise duties have swallowed up the benefit of the savings. According to one study, freight rates dropped by 1–8 per cent.[3] But most traders did not obtain a cut in their freight charges in 1993 and, of the minority which did get a rate reduction, half had to press the road haulage company to get it.[4] Here, those who reaped cost savings from the single market programme have mostly not been able to pass them on in lower prices, though more broadly they may in the end have provided some benefit in terms of improved service.

Certainly, the ending of routine delays at frontiers has helped improve the way that companies warehouse and distribute goods around Europe, and triggered a secondary revolution in logistics, the art or science of moving goods. Companies that used to specialise in customs clearance have been forced to look for other work. Many have become logistics specialists, taking over distribution from traditional wholesalers.[5] The trend for manufacturers to concentrate production on fewer sites has reinforced the scope for centralised distribution. At the same time, the distribution of these products still needs to cater for the differentiated tastes of Europe's consumers and for price differences in various national currencies. So, in the single market, manufacturers can increasingly turn to a new breed of logistic companies, which provide services going far beyond mere delivery of finished goods to retailers. Some logistics companies handle all raw material inputs, as well as finished good outputs for manufacturers, while others have become secondary manufacturers, 'finishing off' goods to suit the tastes of different customers, re-packing them with home language leaflets or national alphabet keyboards, or price-tagging them in different currencies.

All this is producing change in the way goods are dispatched around Europe. The ending of internal border controls and serious delays means that distribution is now less on a country-by-country basis, but resembles more the pattern, long prevalent in the US, of a bicycle wheel with spokes radiating out from a central hub. One result of this is the growth in European Distribution Centres, set up either in-house by big companies or by logistics companies. These EDCs were first developed in the Netherlands, but now appear to be spreading to Belgium, southeast England, the northern, north-eastern and Mediterranean parts of France, Denmark and south-west Sweden (for Scandinavia) and Austria (for eastern Europe). Though mainly used by larger companies, these EDCs appear to be attracting custom from some smaller firms, especially US-owned ones.

Removal of border checks has also given a boost to other logistic techniques such as 'just-in-time' delivery of manufacturing components, 'quick response' replenishment of retail stocks, as well as encouraging the start up of scheduled freight transport services running according to a set timetable. All such techniques and services depend on reliability of delivery as much as sheer speed of delivery. The removal of border checks at last makes it possible to guarantee a certain reliability.

TECHNICAL BARRIERS

The myriad technical rules and regulations on products in Europe have been proved to be far more pervasive barriers to trade than customs controls. Without Community action to remove technical trade barriers, over three-quarters of the value of intra-Community trade in goods would be disrupted by differences between national rules on product specifications. But these barriers cannot be swept away like so many unneeded customs posts. It is essential to have *some* technical regulations to protect the health and safety of consumers and citizens. And it is essential to have *some* technical standards for the smooth operation of commerce and contracting.

But national technical regulations – there were estimated to be 100,000 in the mid-1980s when the EU first began to take seriously the problem of technical barriers to trade – can also be a very effective obstacle to commerce when they have the force of national law behind them. The slightest inconsistency or variation between them can be used by a government, industry or firm of one state to keep out products from other countries – occasionally with justification, usually without.

National regulations which impose technical specifications can be an enormous headache for outside producers. The latter often have to redesign, repackage and re-label their products, go through a complicated registration procedure for such goods as cars, chemicals, pharmaceuticals and foodstuffs and go to the expense of obtaining duplicate test certificates to satisfy local health and safety inspectorates. Rather than face all this, many firms decide to stay at home. Even today, there is less cross-border trade in those sectors which are most subject to technical regulation; these industries account for 33 per cent of gross added value within the EU but only 28 per cent of its trade.[6] Those companies which were not deterred from taking the plunge into a foreign market face a handicap against local firms, because meeting local technical requirements imposed higher production costs and shorter production runs on them. So the new competition tended to be weak competition.

Yet the pointlessness of many of these barriers is clear. For, in demanding that products be tested and often reconfigured in each of their markets, European governments or testing authorities have just been regulating for exactly the same product risks – will this boiler blow up? can that toy injure a child? – in slightly, and often insignificantly, different ways.

It was this reasoning that led the EU to make an assault on technical barriers a major part of its campaign to force a single market and it can now claim considerable success in this very difficult field. Of the 75 per cent of intra-EU trade which is subject to mandatory technical regulations, some major and many minor obstacles have been removed. Take

	Harmonisation of technical regulations and/or standards				Mutual recognition of technical regulations and/or standards				Conformity assessment procedures			
	positive impact	no impact	negative impact	don't know	positive impact	no impact	negative impact	don't know	positive impact	no impact	negative impact	don't know
Food, beverages & tobacco	35	44	9	12	30	48	8	15	24	52	6	19
Machinery & equipment	45	29	20	5	43	37	11	9	32	50	6	12
Electrical & optical machinery	36	48	9	6	50	36	6	8	31	52	8	9
Chemicals, rubber & plastics	33	47	10	10	35	49	7	10	27	53	6	14
Transport equipment	30	56	11	4	49	39	7	5	24	47	5	24
EUR 12	31	51	9	9	32	49	7	12	23	56	5	15

Table 3.1 Impact of single market measures aimed at removing technical barriers

Source: Business survey

cars, as an example of a major improvement. Following the move from separate national systems for authorising sale of a new model in each and every EU market to a single harmonised European 'Whole Type Approval' Directive for the entire European market, manufacturers can now expect to save up to Ecus 30m, or nearly 10 per cent, on the total cost of developing a new car.[7] On a smaller scale, a German toy manufacturer reckons to have saved DM 100,000 in 1995 simply from the way the Toy Safety Directive has eliminated different testing procedures for his products.[8]

Those who have felt most sharply the impact of technical barriers generally see improvement. In the Eurostat survey of business opinion, between 30 and 45 per cent of managers in chemicals, mechanical engineering, office equipment, foodstuffs and motor vehicles said they had gained from the EU effort to remove technical barriers, compared with 20 per cent or less who had experienced negative consequences, probably due to the cost of switching over to new specifications or because of increased competition on their market. Table 3.1 shows the reactions of firms as a whole who responded to the Business survey of the impact of measures to remove technical barriers.

As almost always in this review of the single market's performance, larger companies are more positive than smaller firms about the impact of single market legislation. In the area of technical regulation, this might seem surprising, since most small enterprises find it harder to overcome technical barriers to export markets than big groups do. But most small companies are also relatively recent entrants to export markets, and therefore have less experience of the jungle of technical restrictions that prevailed in Europe a decade ago.

Lower levels of enthusiasm on the part of Small and Medium-sized Enterprises (SMEs) may also reflect their generally more national or local scope. Nevertheless, SMEs in some sectors are positive about the single market. For example, SMEs in the detergent and cosmetics sector have had better access to European markets. And, in the construction machinery sector, 29 per cent of SMEs, as opposed to 7 per cent of large firms, feel that the single market has encouraged them to sell abroad.[9]

Mutual recognition. Much of what progress has been made in recent years is due to a change of strategy, particularly towards a reliance on the principle of mutual recognition. This principle is based on the well-founded assumption that EU states have been regulating for exactly the same products risks. Therefore, they should 'mutually recognise' each other's technical regulations as effectively equivalent in the level of protection they offer consumers. This principle, now well-enshrined in EU law, has proved particularly useful in avoiding the lengthy horse-trading involved in detailed harmonising legislation. In broad economic terms, mutual recognition has been instrumental in overcoming or removing trade barriers affecting more than 25 per cent of intra-EU trade. This figure perhaps underestimates the importance of mutual recognition or acceptance; in areas where member states raise no problems about applying the principle, it is easy to overlook its use. The full potential, too, of mutual recognition is perhaps yet to come in new products, as national testing authorities begin to adopt a gradually more convergent approach to product risks. Figure 3.4 sets out the framework of the mutual recognition principle.

Mutual recognition is not a magical remedy. It works quite well in ensuring that minor differences in capital goods or consumer durables do not become a trade barrier. But – based as it essentially is on mutual trust – it runs up against considerable difficulties on such products as foodstuffs or pesticides where national authorities are understandably worried that, if there is any underlying risk to the product, their consumers will be immediately exposed to it. There are some striking exceptions. For example, in Germany, not a country noted for lax consumer protection, the import and sale of some 200 foods or food additives is permitted, even though their local manufacture is forbidden. But the same sector provides an equally striking example of where achieving mutual recognition is very difficult and the EU market therefore remains fragmented (see box).

Fortified foods and drinks

The addition of vitamins and minerals to foods and drinks is catching on, as Europeans become more health-conscious despite – or perhaps because of – adopting a more sedentary lifestyle and eating more low-nutrition fast food. Yet there are almost no common rules. Four member states – the UK, the Netherlands, Denmark and Sweden – require compulsory restoration in margarine of the vitamins destroyed in its manufacture. France permits restoration of nutrients lost in processing, but requires any fortified foods to be classed as dietetic products. Germany is liberal on vitamins but strict on minerals, while the Netherlands is strict on vitamins but liberal on minerals. Notification procedures are required in Austria, Belgium, Greece, Italy, Luxembourg and the Nordic countries. In addition, significant national variations exist on the type and quantities of nutrients allowed. It would be hard to find a market or series of markets better designed to raise European producers' costs and shorten their production runs.[10]

Mutual recognition can thus make little headway in an area like fortified foodstuffs. The industry's European umbrella organisation, the Confederation des Industries agro-alimentaires, has been canvassing its members about the possible desirability of at least some degree of harmonisation.

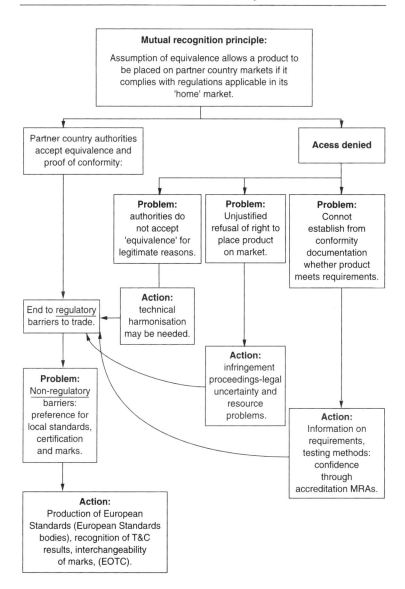

Figure 3.4 Making the mutual recognition principle work

Even where governments allow mutual recognition in theory, there may be insufficient mutual trust or knowledge between their health and safety inspectorates to make it work in practice. And even where it does work in practice, there may be other non-regulatory factors to thwart outsiders. For instance, about half of the products subject to technical regulations of one kind or another are simultaneously affected by the existence of voluntary standards or marks, such as quality marks. In Germany, for example, many customers prefer to see on construction equipment the 'GS' quality mark which, in the past, it was hard for manufacturers outside Germany to obtain.[11] Local buyers tend to hanker after familiar local marks on the goods they buy. This is understandable and there is nothing the EU can, or should do, about this, except first, to ensure that such quality marks are not construed as conferring regulatory approval nor that the absence of such quality marks means absence of regulatory approval, and second, to encourage convergence between these voluntary standards and marks through European-level standardisation.

There is some evidence that mutual recognition works best among a limited subset of member states, essentially neighbours (see box).

Cement is generally regarded as not worth trading across frontiers and certainly not across any great distance, because it is low in value and costly to transport. It is in fact traded quite a lot, because demand for it changes with construction cycles and supply alters with technical factors. The differing geological make-up of cement components across Europe has delayed agreement on a harmonised Euro-standard for cement, though a Construction Products Directive now exists on member states' statute books even if it is not yet properly in force. In the meantime, mutual recognition arrangements exist, but only between Germany, France and the Benelux countries. The real problems appear to confront exporters wanting to sell to countries of which they have limited experience. Thus, northern Europeans complain about southern Europeans, and vice versa (one Spanish producer took 5 months to get a test certificate in Denmark) – but the Portuguese face no obstacles supplying the Spanish market, nor the Dutch the Belgian market.

The task of flattening Europe's technical barriers is made no easier by the fact that new national regulations keep sprouting up. Under a system that requires countries to give notice of new technical rules they propose to make, the member states notified to Brussels some 430–470 new proposed regulations each year during 1992–94, and this in a period when the EU was supposed to be moving towards a common technical environment. All the more surprising is the fact that member states appear to be devoting much of their regulatory energy in precisely those areas where the EU has concentrated its efforts – foodstuffs, transport equipment, chemicals, pharmaceuticals, telecoms equipment, construction products and mechanical engineering.

However, this procedure of notifying proposed new rules gives the Commission and other member states the right to object to any potential trade restrictions they spot in the proposals before the latter become law. They can react by insisting that any new national rule contains a general provision giving mutual recognition rights to partner country products. This may seem of little immediate import to company managers, but it can be of considerable future use to their lawyers, if and when they want to mount a legal challenge to the law in question. From 1997 onward, too, member states will have to notify Brussels and each other of all products where they withhold the benefits of mutual recognition. Not only will this allow better scrutiny of the remaining obstacles, but failure of a member state to raise an objection to a given product will also be read as a signal that it is ready to permit free sale of that product.

Technical harmonisation. The new realisation that mutual recognition has certain limits inevitably gives harmonisation – the quest for identical rules and standards – renewed importance. In truth, however, it was never dropped as a strategy, only modified.

Old-style harmonisation, product-by-product, even component-by-component, is as relevant as ever to products like: cars, medical drugs, chemicals or some foodstuffs, which are considered of potentially high-risk or where evaluation requires EU states to pool their expertise. Here detailed harmonisation has been an arduous business, but, in the view of business and governments alike, worth it. Deeply entrenched technical barriers affecting some 34 per cent of the value of intra-EU trade have, in this painstaking way, been removed.

However, one of the novelties of the single market programme lay in the adoption of another more flexible harmonisation technique, still called the 'new approach' even though it is now ten years old. The idea was simple. To try to speed harmonisation up, it was decided to let those involved concentrate on what they do best. The legislators would legislate the ends to be achieved, the standardisers would standardise the means by which these ends might be achieved. So, member states would confine themselves to setting 'essential requirements' which products would need to meet before being placed on the market. They would then instruct or 'mandate' European standards organisations to come up with harmonised standards. Any manufacturer choosing to follow these standards could benefit from the presumption that his product met the essential requirements, and could effectively 'self-certify' his product. But these standards are not compulsory. They are just an optional technical guideline. A manufacturer is free to opt for other specifications; but if he does so, he needs some independent testing body to certify that his product conforms with the 'essential requirements'. Figure 3.5 shows the 'new approach' to technical harmonisation and how the sequence of events works in practice.[12]

Community efforts to remove barriers are judged to be effective as far as two-thirds of the value of intra-Community trade in products is concerned. This success is mitigated by technical barriers of a non-mandatory nature (such as national standards on conformity) which may require adaptation and retesting of products before they are placed on sale in partner countries. It is estimated that such technical barriers may arise in the case of two out of three products for which regulatory technical barriers have been removed.

As for the remaining third of intra-Community trade in products, it can be divided equally between the areas where there are no apparent technical barriers and those where there are, and where Community rules, either in the form of Directives or the 'mutual recognition' principle, are not judged to be effective. Difficulties can arise, for example, in the interpretation or enforcement of a Directive, or because of delays in the production of harmonised standards which make it easier for manufacturers to follow the rules.

To date, 17 'new approach' Directives, which concern 17 per cent of intra-Community trade, have been adopted; but many have yet to come

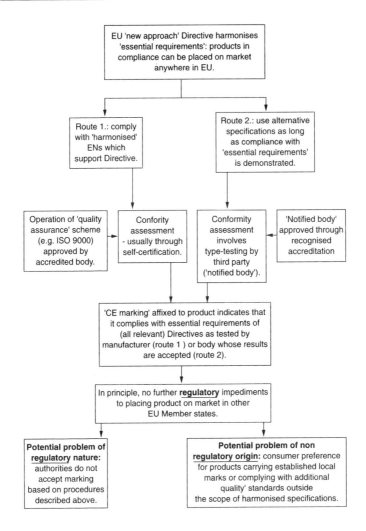

Figure 3.5 Functioning of the 'new approach' to technical harmonisation

into force. For instance, the Toy Safety Directive was the first one to come into effect, on 1 January 1990 and it applied fully from that date, while others have long transition periods. So it is early days to judge the results.

But one problem has become evident. The standardisers have had great difficulty in keeping up with the legislators – but not for want of trying. The European Standardisation Committee, CEN, has no fewer than 500 technical committees at work, while its sister body for electrical-mechanical machinery, CENELEC, has set up 170 working groups. Altogether, the European standards bodies have produced some 5,000 standards, and are working on a further 16,000 – with participants in the member states often now using the Internet to circulate draft texts and modifications and even to vote. But despite such Herculean efforts, they have fallen inevitably behind in some areas. The worst backlog concerns the Machine Safety Directive, where only about 10 per cent of the required 550 accompanying standards have been agreed.

Experience has since shown that manufacturers will only choose 'self certification' for their products where there are clear standards to stick to; to do otherwise might risk product liability suits. Where no agreed Euro-standards are available, a manufacturer has little choice but to devise his own specifications at his own expense and then to go to a certification authority – a Notified Body, in the jargon – for testing. These Notified Bodies usually charge more for testing to a manufacturer's in-house specifications than to a European standard, because they have to design a one-off test for the product. Some Notified Bodies are indeed said to be reluctant to do this kind of testing at all, because they, too, fear that without the backing of a standard some customer might sue them if a product they approved goes wrong.

Experience has also shown that the best results in standardisation seem to come in sectors, like toys, where intra-EU trade is already high, where there is a small number of dominant manufacturers with potential economies of scale that make it possible or advantageous to get a larger slice of the whole EU market. By contrast, in sectors such as cement where any economies of scale can be achieved within national markets and where transport costs are high, companies seem to be unwilling to initiate standards.

PUBLIC PROCUREMENT

Some of the biggest returns from the single market programme were expected from the extension of cross-border competition to public procurement. The expectation was not surprising, given the sums that central and local governments and public utilities spend each year on goods, construction projects and services – Ecus 721 bn in 1994, or 11.5 per cent of the European Union's total output in that year.

This is big money, often in the past spent badly – not in the sense of what it was spent on but *how* it was spent. Out of a general desire to secure jobs and win votes, governments have a strong tendency to reserve contracts to home firms, even though these firms may operate at a sub-optimal level and may not be competitive at the European, let alone world, level.

There could be good reasons for buying locally – lower transport and trading costs, speedier delivery and after-sales service. But aside from the fact that such local advantages are reduced in the single market, they cannot be fully tested and proven unless set against competition from outside suppliers.

So EU legislation in this area has aimed at trying to get governments to adopt the behaviour that comes naturally to private companies and to shop around for the best bargain, which is in the end the best service they can render to their taxpayers. The legislation, beefed up by the single market programme, requires among other things central and local governments and private or public utilities to advertise in the EU's Official Journal and its electronic database, Tenders Electronic Daily (TED), tenders for all contracts above a certain value for goods, projects and services. They must then apply specific rules of procedure which are based on elementary principles, such as: no unfair discrimination, equality of treatment, objectivity and transparency (or openness). Once they have awarded their contracts, these public bodies are then required, in the interests of transparency, to publish the contract awards and the criteria on which they were awarded.

The immediate results[13] of this are encouraging:

- the total number of tender notices in the Official Journal rose from 12,000 in 1987 to more than 95,000 in 1995, with the increase varying from 200 to 900 per cent according to member states;
- armed with this information, some 14–20 per cent of company suppliers to the public sector identified new opportunities in their *domestic* markets, and 9–13 per cent of them went on to win new business as a result;

- some 9–13 per cent of suppliers spotted new opportunities in *other* EU states and 3–4 per cent won extra business as a result.

There are other results[14] which are equally encouraging (but are also the consequence of broad economic factors like recession, technology change, restructuring, mergers and takeovers affecting particularly the capital goods sector):

- public sector purchases of non-domestic origin rose from 6 per cent in 1987 to 10 per cent in 1994. Imports sold directly across borders increased from 1.4 to 3 per cent. Most of the increase was in indirect imports (sold through local subsidiaries or agents) which rose from 4 to 7 per cent of total public procurement over the same period. This last increase reflects the trend of bigger companies in telecommunications, power equipment and railway rolling stock to swallow up smaller companies in other EU states;
- competitiveness, as measured by the EU's trade balance with the rest of the world, increased in power transformers, X-ray equipment and telecoms switching equipment. In this last sector, the EU trade surplus rose from Ecus 250m in 1988 to Ecus 900m in 1994;
- prices fell by 20–30 per cent for telecoms equipment and railway rolling stock, and by 30–40 per cent for electrical equipment. This was inevitably of benefit to public budgets and taxpayers. But it was partly or mainly due to downward pressures on prices exerted by recession, over-capacity in these industries and the squeeze on public procurement budgets as much as to EU public procurement Directives.

These Directives built on the EU's first attempts in the 1970s to open up public procurement to competitive cross-border bidding. But the effort was incomplete; the Directives only applied to public works, like buildings, or supplies, like uniforms or paper. So the new single market Directives of the late 1980s added in services, like municipal garbage collection, and included the very important utility sectors of telecommunications, water, energy and transport.

Enforcement. Some of these Directives are fairly recent: three of them entered into force in mid 1994. The Utilities Directive has yet to come into force in Greece, and Portugal. But, as we have seen in Chapter 2, even when they enter into force, the Directives are not always incorporated into national law. The Commission is consequently pursuing some member states for failing to transpose the Directives into their national law, as it pursues those who have failed to do so correctly. Even when the right legal framework is all in place, there is the problem of policing it. This task falls chiefly to the Commission, not least because there is anecdotal evidence that, even where they feel they have been unfairly discriminated against, many contractors are shy of offending potential customers by trying to take public authorities to court.

In the past, public authorities have used a variety of ruses to dodge the Directives' impact. These tactics include splitting up contracts into smaller lots, each of which fall below the value threshold requiring open tendering; specifying national technical standards or local firms' proprietary products in tenders; demanding more financial or technical requirements of foreign companies than local firms; giving first-time bidders insufficient time to respond to tenders; and bogusly classifying contracts as 'continuations' of previous contracts, or as 'emergency' procurements so as to exploit loopholes in the EU Directives and so escape advertising.

It is possible that some public authorities are still using such tactics. Certainly, there is a discrepancy between the number of public bodies who probably *ought* to be advertising their contracts, and the number which *actually* do so. The number of EU public bodies or utilities which are covered by the legislation and which are of a size to award contracts big enough to exceed the value thresholds in the Directives is estimated at 110,000.[15] But the number which advertised contracts last year was only around 16,500, about 15 per cent. Back in 1993, one tenth of Europe's towns with a population of over 100,000 and nearly one third of towns of 50,000–100,000 inhabitants, publicised no contracts whatsoever.

Perceptions. There are some striking examples of how public procurers have benefited from the market-broadening – and mind-broadening – effect of international contract tendering. One public buyer was able to buy from another EU state, electrical equipment that was 50 per cent cheaper (because of a different technical solution) than what was on offer from his domestic companies. In another case, a railway authority ended up buying rolling stock from a supplier in another EU state which the authority had never heard of until the supplier replied to the authority's tender notice in the Official Journal.

Sector/Product	NACE	% OJ readership[1]	% which won new domestic business[2]	% which won new other, EU business[3]	Public sector import penetration (%)[4] 1994	
					direct	indirect
Low-tech products						
Office furniture	316	34	9	2	5	8
Uniforms	453	47	12	4	3	13
Printing and paper	471/2	26	6	0	1	17–19
High-tech products with common tech. specs.						
Office machinery	33	45	17	3	4	22–29
Motor vehicles	351	41	12	3	3–4	16–19
Medical equip.	37	26	10	2	5–6	19–21
High-tech products with different tech. specs.						
Boilers	315	31	12	4	4	9–10
Power generating equip.	341/2	42	10	4	6–7	11–14
Telecomm. equip.	344	42	13	7	6–8	18–22
Railway rolling stock	362	49	12	10	10–11	19–21
Works						
Construction/civil eng.	502	44	11	4	3	4–7
Services						
Consulting engineering	83	52	22	4	1	5–6
EU average		41	9–13	3–4	2–4	5–9

Table 3.2 Supplier response and public sector import penetration

Sources: 1. Procurement Study (Figure 13.2)
2. % of suppliers to the public sector winning additional domestic business (Figure 13.12)
3. % of suppliers to the public sector winning additional business in other EU Member States (Figure 13.23)
4. Table 1.1.31.

But many public procurement authorities profess a certain disappointment that their contract advertisements have not drawn enough new bids, or sufficiently competitive bids. Part of the trouble may be that companies from other EU states are often bidding through their local subsidiaries, which in turn tend to price their offers in line with the domestic competition. It is notable that the two successful bids mentioned above – on electrical equipment and railway rolling stock – were by suppliers selling direct from another member state. Table 3.2 from the Procurement study shows the picture for supplier response and public sector import penetration in 1994.

Larger companies appear to be gaining the most from the new system. They are more likely to read the OJ or tap into TED, and more likely to win new business in both domestic and non-domestic markets as a result than smaller firms are. This is predictable. Larger companies have more manpower to scan tender notices for business opportunities and a wider range of goods and services potentially to fill those opportunities. However, those small and medium-sized firms which used the OJ and TED were as successful as their bigger brethren in winning business in at least domestic markets. And it is this greater intensity of domestic competition that may be one of the least anticipated, but most significant, benefits of the new EU measures.

Trade flows. To use the categories in the EU Directives, import penetration has increased more in supplies than in works or services, with any increase in the latter coming as a result of a few large international construction projects and their related services provided by architects and consultant engineers. Among goods deemed to be 'procurement sensitive' – because it is mainly governments who have the money or use for them – the highest import penetration has occurred in those goods with a relatively high technology content, railway rolling stock, medical equipment, office machinery and telecoms equipment. The main beneficiaries of this increased trade are Germany, France and to a lesser extent the UK and Italy. But many of these imports are indirect, in the sense of being made locally by subsidiaries of companies based in other EU states. This reflects the restructuring in many high-tech sectors, with the few remaining big groups buying up other companies or establishing themselves in other member states (see box, p. 38).

Telecoms equipment. This is now dominated by three globally competitive companies – Alcatel of France, Siemens of Germany and Ericsson of Sweden who have all taken over a number of smaller companies in other countries in recent years. As a result the degree of import penetration in intra-EU telecoms trade by direct imports was only 6 per cent in 1994, but indirect imports supplied by local subsidiaries or affiliates accounted for a further 19 per cent of the market.

Railway rolling stock. This is again dominated by three groups – Siemens, the Franco-British joint company of GEC-Alsthom and the Adtranz joint venture of ABB (the Swiss-Swedish group) and of AEG of Germany. All have a strong presence in other member states. GEC-Alsthom, for example, manufactures in Austria, Belgium, Italy, Germany as well as in France and the UK. In 1994 direct imports accounted for 10 per cent of intra-EU trade, and indirect imports for another 20 per cent.

Power generation equipment. Five companies – GEC-Alsthom, Siemens, ABB, Fiat and Ansaldo of Italy – have 80 per cent of the market. In intra-EU trade, direct imports took 5 per cent of the market, and indirect imports, 13 per cent in 1994.

Prices. The disappearance of buy-at-home habits, plus the removal of technical barriers, was expected to produce a convergence of prices of many goods bought by the public sector. There is little evidence of this happening over the 1987–94 period, except in cardiac monitors, buses and office machinery. Exchange rate movements and inflation differences partly explain the failure of prices to move together. Certainly, as we have seen, some prices have moved downwards, sometimes very sharply. But other economic factors are as responsible for this as the single market programme.

Now that we have taken a look across the board, we can sum up the overall position as far as barriers are concerned. Today's single market is a world away from the old days when all goods were stopped and checked at borders. Border controls have been completely abolished and businesses across Europe say that they are already reaping the benefits. The single market legislation has also assured the free movement of most products and the new regulatory system is generally welcomed. But, as we have seen, there is still some way to go before all the barriers are completely removed. Only complete implementation of the remaining Directives will enable full exploitation and appropriation of the benefits. It's true that 'mutual recognition' is difficult to apply in practice but the problem is being addressed. More European standards are also needed to help get rid of non-regulatory obstacles to market access. Willingness on the part of companies to think and operate in new ways that will exploit the single market's opportunities, are crucial to success.

So it is up to governments to take mutual recognition seriously and down to business to help make the new standards if it wants a fully functional single market. That will only happen when national governments, and businesses themselves, decide to play the game seriously.

Notes

[1] Customs & frontiers.
[2] Idem.
[3] Road freight.
[4] Customs & frontiers.
[5] Impact of Internal Market Integration on Organisation and Performance of Distribution, Coopers & Lybrand 1996.
[6] Technical Barriers.
[7] Vehicles.
[8] Technical Barriers.
[9] Business Survey.
[10] Technical Barriers.
[11] Construction.
[12] Technical Barriers.
[13] Procurement.
[14] Procurement.
[15] Procurement.

Chapter 4

Milestones in Manufacturing

It is time now to look more closely at how individual industries have been affected by the elimination or reduction of some of the 'horizontal' obstacles to trade – ie problems faced by most sectors – discussed in the previous chapter as well as by single market legislation designed to remove barriers specific to those sectors. By examining some of the detail, we can get more of a feel for the impact of the single market programme on the ground, before taking a broader view of its wider effects in later chapters.

We start with manufacturing, because it is here that many of the longest-lasting barriers have existed and here that EU efforts to remove barriers began even before the single market programme. But before doing so, it is worth bearing in mind how services, the focus of the next chapter, interact with manufacturing.

A service like road transport is vital to all manufacturers. It is thus not surprising that deregulation of road freight is rated as one of the single market's main successes with 43 per cent of firms surveyed claiming it had a positive impact on their business. Services can not only have this supply-side effect of increasing manufacturers' ability to reach customers across the Union; they can also stimulate demand for products. New telecoms services use new telecoms equipment. A more pan-European approach in a service sector like advertising can also create more pan-European demand for goods.

Some generalities about the single market's impact on manufacturing can be extracted from polling evidence. Table 4.1 shows what firms who responded to the Business survey thought.

Industry sector	Firms				Firm break-down	Employees				Employee break-down	Turnover				Turnover break-down
	+	0	-	?		+	0	-	?		+	0	-	?	
Food products & beverages 15	30	48	8	15	20.9	33	47	7	12	20.4	32	49	6	13	30.0
Tobacco products 16	30	50	0	20	0.1	55	29	0	16	0.5	60	27	0	13	0.8
Textiles & clothing 17+18	17	61	7	15	22.2	25	60	3	12	14.5	24	62	2	11	7.3
Chemicals & chemical products 24	37	47	4	12	6.9	47	38	2	13	13.6	48	37	2	13	17.3
Fabricated metal products 28	32	55	4	9	22.0	36	54	5	6	14.2	36	55	4	5	11.5
Machinery & equipment NEC 29	43	37	11	9	20.8	48	37	8	7	20.7	49	37	8	7	16.0
Office mach. & computers 30	31	63	0	5	2.5	41	50	0	9	2.5	42	48	0	10	2.2
Motor veh., trailers 34	43	44	8	4	4.7	52	36	7	5	13.4	51	36	7	5	14.9

Table 4.1 Impact of the single market

Source: Eurostat

Manufacturers are more upbeat about the single market than service companies. Of the 13,500 companies which responded to the 1995 Eurostat Business Survey, 41 per cent of manufacturing firms said the single market programme had been successful in eliminating obstacles to EU trade in their sector, compared to only 22 per cent of service companies which thought likewise. However, manufacturers were more cautious when asked the question: 'Has the single market programme been a success for your firm?' Only a third answered yes. By nationality, manufacturers from the periphery – Mediterranean countries and Ireland – were more positive than those from more centrally-placed countries. By size, larger companies say they have benefited more than smaller ones – who may of course be less likely to trade across borders.

In fact, global 'models' – simplified simulations of reality – using evidence from various studies shows benefits all round. For example, prices of highly traded consumer and equipment goods have converged across the EU. This is mainly due to changes in market structures and competition prompted by the single market programme. Models and types of consumer goods on offer are also more similar, thanks to the single market measures. In 1980, EU prices for identical goods varied by 26 per cent for consumer goods and 18 per cent for equipment goods. By 1993, this variance had fallen to 19.5 and 14.5 per cent respectively.

To get a more precise view of the single market's impact, one has to delve into more sectoral detail. The six case studies examined below – telecommunications equipment, processed food, cars, chemicals, pharmaceuticals, textiles and construction equipment – represent 38 per cent of the EU's industrial output and 43 per cent of its total added value.

TELECOMS EQUIPMENT

The telecommunications equipment industry is Europe's third biggest, with an annual turnover of around Ecus 35bn and employment of over 700,000. But only in recent years has it become one of its most competitive. It has slashed its prices, raised its exports and with GSM mobile phone technology developed what is fast becoming a world standard.

Credit for this can by no means be attributed wholly to the single market programme. Technology has helped, in particular the arrival of digital integrated circuits, which are cheaper to manufacture and more reliable to use, and of fibre optic cables capable of carrying more data. So did the world-wide move towards telecoms deregulation. Inside the EU this started a decade ago in the UK and (among new EU members) Sweden.

But the EU has matched this world-wide trend with its own liberalising legislation, creating a positive feedback between what was happening at the level of the EU and of member states. This EU legislation specifically directed at equipment included:

- ending the monopoly rights of national telephone operators to dictate what terminal equipment like faxes or modems could be attached to their lines;
- mutual recognition of 'type approval' of telecommunications equipment, which therefore became cheaper and easier to sell in all member states;
- creation of the European Telecommunications Standards Institute (ETSI) which has reduced technical incompatibilities between systems.

Matching this in services have been the moves to:

- end by 1998 national telephone operators' monopoly right to provide ordinary voice telephony and build telecom infrastructures;
- rules to guarantee new telecoms service providers open access to public networks;
- freedom for new operators to provide mobile phone services using the GSM mobile phone standard which has now been adopted by 138 operators in 77 countries.

All these measures have forced the old national telephone operators, who account for 80 per cent of all telecoms equipment purchases, to change their buying habits. In this new competitive world, they have simply had to get the best price and quality from their supplier. In the past, this supplier always used to be the national telecom equipment manufacturer, where one existed. So France Telecom always went to Alcatel, Deutsche Telekom to Siemens, and so on. This automatic link between national operator and national supplier no longer exists. The tendency of EU operators to buy a large share of their switching and transmission equipment from their traditional sources has not disappeared overnight. But liberalisation has strengthened competition between traditional suppliers and opened the way for new companies to enter the market, particularly network suppliers from the US and terminal equipment suppliers from Asia.

	1985	1995	CAGR (real)
Public switching			
Competitive world price (1995 ECU)	420	170	−9%
EU maximum price (1995 ECU)	820	260	−11%
EU minimum price (1995 ECU)	450	170	−9%
EU median price (1995 ECU)	670	210	−11%
EU average price premium	60%	24%	
Transmission equipment			
Competitive world price per channel			
(1985 = 100)	100	2.4	−31%
EU maximum price per channel (index)	160	3.2	−32%
EU minimum price per channel (index)	130	2.4	−33%
EU median price per channel (index)	138	2.6	−33%
EU average price premium	38%	5%	
Customer premises equipment			
Competitive world price (1985 = 100)	100	39	−9%
EU maximum price (index)	180	58	−11%
EU minimum price (index)	130	40	−11%
EU median price (index)	152	49	−11%
EU average price premium (index)	52%	25%	
Approximate overall average			
price premium	50%	20%	
'Corrected' price premium[1]	20%	8%	

Table 4.2 Estimated EU equipment price premiums, 1985–95

Source: Telecom. equipment[2]
[1]   See Chapter 7, footnote 15 of Cecchini (1988).
[2]   1995 figures were derived from an Analysys survey of industry contacts and synthesis of known contract terms.

This has exerted enormous downward pressure on prices. A decade ago EU telecoms equipment prices were estimated[1] to be at least 20 per cent above the most competitive world level (usually US). This premium over US levels is now greatly reduced.

In general, this progressive reduction in the 'excess' of EU prices over US levels has benefited EU customers – be they national telephone operators or individual Europeans – by some Ecus 3.5 bn a year over the past decade of 1985–95. By no means all of this is thanks to the single market measures. But perhaps half of it is.

Stripping out the many other factors at work in the European telecommunications industry, research has estimated that if the EU had not taken the liberalising steps that it did, European customers would have foregone average equipment price reductions of approximately 7 per cent – equivalent to an annual extra cost of Ecus 1.5–2bn to European equipment buyers.

The equipment manufacturers could hardly be expected to welcome such sharp price reductions. But generally they have offset lower margins on their products by reaping economies of scale across the enlarged single market through higher output and exports. Their exports outside the EU rose from Ecus 4bn in 1988 to Ecus 7bn in 1993, while the EU's trade surplus with the rest of the world in this sector rose from virtually zero to Ecus 1.5bn over the same period.

Since the EU's major competitors have benefited from roughly the same technical advances as the EU itself, it is a fair supposition that much of this improved trade balance is due to improved competitiveness spurred on by the liberalisation in telecommunications services. Research confirms[2] that *in the absence of the single market programme*, EU telecoms equipment output would be about Ecus 1bn less than it currently is.

MOTOR VEHICLES

The car industry differs from telecoms and most other sectors in that it is possible to attribute some very precise savings directly to the single market programme, while the indirect impact of the broader EU measures has had relatively little effect on an industry that has long organised itself to operate across Europe's borders.

The cost savings flow from a belated success in technical harmonisation. Cars and their components have long, for obvious safety reasons, been clear candidates for straight harmonisation at a considerable level of detail. Starting in 1970, negotiators agreed common requirements for more than 40 different car components. But for a long time the attempt to agree a harmonised approval test for an entire car – or 'whole type approval' – was frustrated by some countries and car industries who worried that outsiders, especially the Japanese, would benefit more than they themselves from the freedom of marketing that such whole type approval would bring. Eventually, after a trade arrangement was agreed with Japan in 1991, whole type approval was agreed in 1992 and came into effect for new models in 1996.

As a result a car approved in one EU state is automatically authorised for sale in all the others. The new system is not only easier but cheaper. Research[3] estimates that car manufacturers may be now able to save up to 10 per cent of the cost of developing a new model (for the arithmetic of this, see below).

Car test savings

The savings come in two forms – hardware and time:

- each test of a new car involves the destruction of three versions of the new model to see how the new car stands up to the impact of a crash from the front, rear and side. Test 15 times (in each member state), and you destroy 45 cars. Test once, and you only destroy three cars and save from demolition 42 others whose value is put at an average of Ecus 1 m;

- the length of national approval tests has varied according to country, about 3 months in the UK but 6 months in Germany. The effect of one-stop approval will be for approval procedures to converge towards the speediest, or at least for manufacturers to have the choice of opting for the speediest. The research, design and development costs of a new car are around Ecus 400m and the process takes about 36 months. If that process is shortened by 3 months, you save the cost of keeping your development team active for that extra time and you save up to Ecus 30m.

By contrast, the broader aspects of the single market programme have had relatively little impact on Europe's car industry at a time when it was already undergoing important changes as a result of globalisation, improved working methods (often borrowed from Japan) and a deep recession. The EU measures have made it easier for new entrants, chiefly Japanese and Korean, to compete on equal terms with existing manufacturers. This has therefore increased the level of competition, which has so far shown itself in more choice and service for consumers rather than in lower prices.

The single market programme has not changed the pattern of trade in finished cars. Intra-EU trade has remained fairly stable, at a high rate; as a proportion of total registrations in the EU, those assembled in another EU country account for slightly over 50 per cent. Imports from outside the EU have increased slightly, mainly due to the arrival of Korean companies in 1991 and their capture of about 2 per cent of the market. Japanese companies have increased their share of the EU market from 9 per cent in 1988 to 11 per cent in 1994, but the increase has been almost entirely with cars made in the UK through investment undoubtedly attracted by the single market.

However, the removal of border delays and the deregulation of road freight seem to have encouraged companies – both assemblers and component-makers – to reap the advantages of implanting themselves in lower cost countries around the EU's periphery. Most of the investments have been in areas of Spain, Portugal, the UK and Italy which have not traditionally made cars, though some have also gone into central Europe in expectation of the EU's enlargement to the east.

The single market programme appears to have little effect on production, as distinct from R&D costs, while measured across the EU as a whole the variations in final prices of cars are (slightly) wider than ever. These price differentials are caused chiefly by currency fluctuations and tax. Member states still tax cars very differently- six countries base vehicle purchase tax on cubic capacity of engines, four on weight, two on levels of horsepower and two on the type of fuel used.

PROCESSED FOODSTUFFS

No industry has been more beset by technical barriers than processed foodstuffs. Nearly 100 of the original White Paper's 282 Directives applied to the food industry. Removing these barriers and getting EU-wide agreement on ingredients, processing, packaging, labelling and marketing has been difficult. Even where harmonisation directives are agreed, member states have often been slow to transpose them into national law. The mutual recognition principle has had its part to play in the agreement that there is no harm – indeed positive benefit in terms of consumer choice – in foods having different ingredients, provided that these ingredients are clearly pointed out to the consumer on the label. But some member states have tended to require manufacturers to put more detail on the label than the Labelling Directive demanded.

Yet, overall, the industry seems generally positive about the limited progress made. Of companies which responded to an industry-wide survey, 96 out of 108 said the single market programme had either 'significantly' or 'to some extent' removed trade barriers.[4] A combination of some harmonisation and mutual recognition has helped companies in some sectors to realise economies of scale and scope. They can more easily manufacture according to a single recipe rather than maintain lots of parallel recipes for different national markets. The resulting cost reductions tended to be seized by the small number of very big companies in the industry more easily than by the large number of small niche manufacturers which characterise this industry.

The varied nature of this sector makes generalisation hard. One of the biggest increases in intra-EU trade came in what are classified for customs as 'other foods', a heterogeneous category mainly of coffee, tea, soups, sauces, condiments, whose only common factor is that they are of relatively high value compared to their bulk and therefore to their transport cost. Sharing the same high value to bulk ratio, cross-border sales of spirits and chocolate also increased. But there has also always been considerable intra-EU trade in spirits because they are relatively standard products and because in each case their production is concentrated in a few member states. By contrast, in products like beer, soft drinks, mineral water and pasta, the single market has not seen any real increase in intra-EU trade because of local preferences (in the case of beer and drinks) or of ingredients (like the durum wheat which Italians insist should go into pasta). Not surprisingly in such a variegated market, there is little evidence of price convergence, except to some limited extent in soft drinks and also in Greece, Spain and Portugal, undoubtedly a catch-up effect of their relatively recent entry into the EU.

CHEMICALS

Single market legislation has reduced obstacles to trade, helped the chemical industry exploit its considerable economies of scale, increased competition and concentration and led intra-EU trade to rise relative to total trade. But – in contrast to most other sectors – the EU measures, particularly accompanying legislation on pollution control and waste management, have increased industry's short-term costs.

With the Single European Act (1986) providing the basis for environmental legislation, environmental protection became a key element in the construction of the single market. Partly as a result, industry in the EU found itself by the early 1990s spending more on environmental protection as a share of capital spending than in the US or Japan – as can be seen from Figure 4.1. But the evidence is that this did not of itself lead to a loss of international sales because environmental costs are a relatively small share of the total. In surveys a number of companies stressed the benefits of EU-wide environmental measures in creating a level playing field, quite apart from the long-term welfare benefits for all – see Chapter 9 for more on environmental issues.

Elsewhere, the single market programme acted on industry's costs in both directions. New harmonised regulations and certification procedures pushed up the short term costs of chemical companies, which nonetheless shared in the general benefit to industry of quicker, cheaper transport as a result of the disappearance of border delays and freight deregulation.

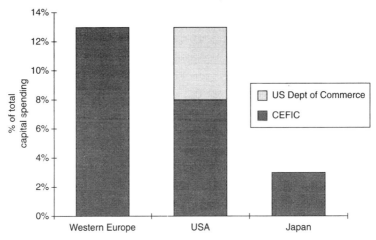

Figure 4.1 Chemical industry capital spending on environmental protection

Source: CEFIC, US Department of Commerce survey

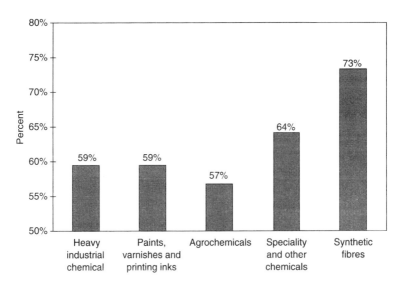

Figure 4.2 Intra-EC exports as a percentage of total exports, 1993

Source: Eurostat. DEBA

Intra-EU trade rose as a share of total trade (though this is partly due to a fall in the European chemical sector's trade balance with other major trading blocks) see Figures 4.2 and 4.3. Competition increased, particularly in southern Europe, while there was a general increase in merger and acquisition activity across the EU. This in turn led to more concentration in the industry, but this does not appear to have had any detrimental effect because of the simultaneous impact of the single market programme on competition, through easier market access and increased intra-EU trade.

As to the future, the chemical industry is far from alone in wanting to see a greater degree of tax harmonisation and an end to trade-distorting currency fluctuations. But it has signalled a particular interest in a more consistent approach to environmental protection and in a freer energy market. Large amounts of energy go into making chemicals and the industry welcomes the prospect of cheaper supplies flowing from the energy liberalisation agreed in June 1996.

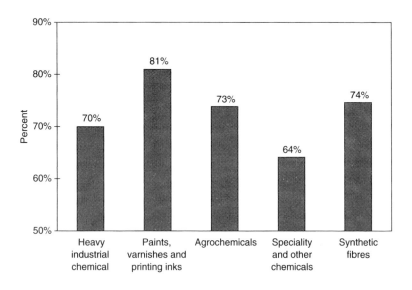

Figure 4.3 Intra-EC imports as a percentage of total imports, 1993
Source: Eurostat. DEBA

CONSTRUCTION SITE EQUIPMENT

The characteristic of this industry is that while a few companies specialise at a global level and make the most common types of excavator in long production runs, most manufacture is in small batches or even single items. A lot of cranes or 'off-highway' equipment like bulldozers, bucket loaders, graders and road rollers are tailored to the customer.

This limits opportunities for making economies of scale in the single market. At the same time, the large number of variants and specialist equipment produced by some manufacturers, especially smaller niche producers, has made the business of getting national type approval costly and time-consuming. This has made EU Directives, like the Machinery Directive and the Electromagnetic Compatibility Directive of 1989 which create a one-stop type approval for the EU market, particularly relevant to this sector. But, generally, these Directives still lack harmonised standards produced by standards bodies to make them fully effective.

Most companies have welcomed these measures taken so far to reduce technical barriers. But as Table 4.3 shows, they are in two minds about the Directives' effect, even though the longer term benefits of technical standardisation will last longer than the largely one-off cost of complying with the new Directives.

The majority agreed the measures helped improve the quality of their machines, but only about one in six believed that this had helped make their products more competitive or encouraged them to sell in world markets. This was because three-quarters judged that the EU Directives had raised the cost of their products. And some manufacturers went on to complain that over-regulation was costing them business in many markets outside the EU which only required basic equipment with little regard for safety.

The views of companies are naturally coloured by the cycle of the construction industry which after a long period (1984-90) of growth has gone into an equally long decline since 1990. Inside the EU, demand has held up fairly well. But EU production has fallen because while extra-EU exports have also decreased, imports from the rest of the world have stayed steady. As a result, the ratio of extra-EU exports to imports fell from 5:1 in 1981 to 1.5:1 in 1992.

	Yes	No	No response
Improved quality of your products	55%	34%	11%
Increased product costs	74%	16%	9%
Technical problems in meeting legislative requirements	53%	36%	11%
Making your products more competitive in the EU	16%	65%	19%
Encouraging you to sell in other world markets	18%	52%	30%

Base: all, n = 74

Table 4.3 'Have these directives contributed to the following?'

In this climate, EU manufacturers have tended to be on the defensive, protecting their market position rather than expanding it across EU borders. Nonetheless, competition has increased in the single market, partly because of imports, with the market share of the top five producers in the EU falling from 50.3 per cent in 1988 to 42.7 per cent in 1994. In order to try to stay competitive, construction equipment makers have taken advantage of freer movement of goods around the EU to source their components more widely. Over 40 per cent of firms reported they had revised their purchasing policy as a result of the single market measures.

TEXTILES AND CLOTHING

Textiles and clothing fall into the category which marketing men call 'fast moving consumer goods'. They need to move fast in response to fashion and demand – and they are indeed moving faster as a result of the removal of border delays.

This has cut the average time between orders and deliveries by 15–20 per cent, a finding confirmed more generally in the distribution sector. Manufacturers can give their retailers not only a quicker service but also a more flexible one, because lower transport costs appear to make them readier to supply in small batches. Companies reckon the absence of border checks and delays has cut an average 10 per cent off their transport costs. These costs are typically 2–5 per cent of sales, so the transport saving is equivalent to 0.2–0.5 per cent of total turnover. Textile and clothing firms claim that abolition of the old system of organising cross-border shipments has saved them anywhere between 0.08 and 0.6 per cent in of turnover, though some of this saving has been wiped out by the new system for reporting trade statistics.[5]

To a degree only shared by the car industry, national textile industries in the EU used to depend on intra-EU border checks to protect themselves from *indirect* imports (ie coming from India to France via Belgium). These intra-EU controls on textile imports finally disappeared at the start of 1995 to be replaced by EU-wide quotas on textile imports administered at the EU's external frontiers. Textile and clothing companies have not fared too badly, however.

Imports have risen. The share of the EU textile market taken by imports from outside the EU increased from 13.6 per cent in 1986 to 25.6 per cent in 1994, while for clothing, the proportion of outside imports rose from 15.6 to 33.4 per cent over the same period. But because competition is more on price rather than on quality, EU industry has generally switched to higher value products. Counterfeiting remains a problem, but the EU introduced common legislation against this in 1995.

However, there are still technical barriers within the market. Some 24 technical standards have been agreed, but some 170 more are still being drafted. As a result, manufacturers still have to resort to country-by-country testing of their goods for inflammability, for certain banned chemical substances and for use by the construction industry.

PHARMACEUTICALS

Europe's pharmaceutical market still remains fragmented along national lines, chiefly because it is subject to price controls which national governments impose through what their health insurance schemes choose to reimburse patients.

Nonetheless, there is now:

- the European Medicines Evaluation Agency, set up in 1995, to coordinate the authorisation of new drugs on the market;
- the Transparency Directive of 1989 which requires governments to be quicker to take decisions on prices and reimbursement on drugs and to explain the decisions they have taken;
- the 'rational use of medicines' Directives of 1992, which create common rules on how drugs are advertised and what information is given to patients.

This has helped increase intra-EU trade. Cross-border trade in retail finished medicines rose from 9.8 per cent of total consumption in 1988 to 17.2 per cent in 1994, and the growth in this cross-border trade has been above the EU average in southern countries – France, Greece, Italy and especially Spain. Table 4.4 shows the size of this increase.

Thus, EU actions have helped somewhat towards unifying the market and providing the means of supplying it. But it is surprising that cross border trade is not higher, given the price gaps between national markets. Some trading takes place in parallel to that organised by manufac-

	1988	1989	1990	1991	1992	1993	1994
B	42.1	45.6	45.0	47.0	50.9	47.7	56.8
D	6.7	8.5	9.0	9.5	9.9	9.2	11.0
DK	39.2	38.4	37.0	41.2	46.7	32.6	43.3
E	2.6	3.8	4.2	5.1	8.5	11.5	15.3
F	4.6	5.6	6.7	7.8	8.3	8.3	8.9
GR	15.9	21.8	29.0	25.8	31.6	27.5	29.6
I	5.0	5.2	5.7	5.7	7.3	8.7	10.8
IRL	75.1	90.8	91.8	92.7	92.6	78.8	87.2
NL	53.8	58.9	58.6	59.8	62.1	61.6	82.3
P	16.0	13.8	15.3	13.7	16.6	16.7	18.5
UK	15.2	18.2	17.5	18.8	19.1	18.6	21.1
EU	9.8	11.2	11.6	12.2	13.6	13.9	17.2

Table 4.4 Imports of finished medicines from other EU member nations as a percentage of consumption (1988–94)

Source: Eurostat Nace 257 database

turers and their main distributors – mainly buying in low priced markets (Belgium, France, Italy, Spain) and selling in higher priced ones (Denmark, Germany, Netherlands, the UK). But this form of arbitrage is still very small, accounting for only 4 per cent of the consumption of prescription drugs.

Cross-border marketing of drugs remains difficult, despite the 1992 Directives which went as far as member states were able to agree at that time. Member states' practices vary, according to what they deem to be a prescription drug and what advertisements they will allow. Selling pharmaceutical products by mail order – a form of marketing which has taken 10 per cent of the US market – is illegal in several EU states, while in the Netherlands even prescription pharmaceutical products can be sold in this way.

The research-based end of the pharmaceutical industry is, not surprisingly, concerned about any increase in parallel trading. R&D costs as a share of sales have risen in the EU from 9.3 per cent in 1982 to 12.3 per cent in 1993. Some potential economies exist in R&D. There are no less than 128 R&D plants in the EU outside the company's country of origin, even though the evidence is that most breakthroughs come in a company's home base. Rationalisation of R&D, as well as of production sites, is now occurring, but mainly through the mega-mergers which are driven more by global than EU competition.

Overall, in spite of the fact that it is still early days, it is possible to see and measure the actual advances achieved in manufacturing. Of course, these are only milestones along the way, rather than arrival at the desired destination. Manufacturing still stands to benefit further from all of the action being taken to improve the application and enforcement of the rules and the provision of the necessary standards. This is because the fact that one is dealing with tangible identifiable products makes the whole exercise fairly concrete. However, the story is not quite so straightforward for services.

Notes

[1] Cecchini report.
[2] Telecom. equipment.
[3] Vehicles.
[4] Foodstuffs.
[5] Textiles.

Chapter 5

Breaking New Ground in Services

The single market programme was the first serious assault on barriers to the provision of services across the EU. It was the first attempt because services are generally a more recent economic activity to develop than manufacturing and because services are a more complicated area, due to the contractual relationship between supplier and customer. At the same time there was a serious need to liberalise services because they form the fastest growing part of the European economy.

Trade in services takes place through the use of international services, such as when you send your goods in a truck to a neighbouring country, or telephone abroad, or hire a foreign architect. Or through, as economists would say, the international movement of production factors like capital or labour, such as when you make a money transfer through your bank or set up an after-sales company abroad to service goods like cars. Or through consumption of foreign 'non-traded' services, as a tourist might when he stays in a foreign hotel or eats in a foreign restaurant. These latter services are still called 'non-traded' because the service-provider – the hotelier or restaurateur – can not bring his hotel or restaurant to you.

But the definition of what is non-traded is shrinking with the advent of the single market. Municipal garbage collection might, for instance, have been regarded as typically non-traded. Under the opening up of public procurement, however, a town council in one EU state might well award the contract to collect its garbage to a company based in another member state.

Member states have spun a web of regulatory restrictions around services, for several reasons. In banking, insurance, road and air transport, they have often sought to ensure market stability, or safety, or consumer protection in ways which create significant barriers to cross-border trade and/or discriminate against outside operators. In telecommunications, audio-visual services, and again in air transport, they have invoked the requirements of public service and/or the physical limitations of a network to award special or exclusive rights, ownership rules, or restrictions on broadcasting frequencies which have had the effect of limiting competition and denying access to outsiders. In professional and business services, obstacles to cross-border trade have stemmed from member states' different requirements for people like architects, engineers, lawyers, management consultants, and so on, to exercise their profession in another member state.

The single market programme in services started slowly but has gathered pace. It began in what people regarded as traditional services – banking, insurance and transport. Telecommunications services were added and, subject to the approval of the European Parliament, electricity will be added soon. Among newer technologies, the single market programme tackled audio-visual services from the outset, but is only now confronting the explosive growth in on-line information services which have opened new ways of selling across Europe's borders. Partly because of this phased timetable, the progress has been significant in liberalising transport and financial services, but more modest in other service sectors.

Before examining this in sectoral detail, it is worth noting that, just as we saw in the last chapter, some service sectors have had a powerful influence on manufacturing. Some of the single market measures targeted at improving the flow of goods across borders have also had powerful ramifications for services.

This is obvious in the case of road transport, where the removal of internal border delays has enabled hauliers to save, on average, 5 per cent of their total costs on a typical intra-EU journey of 1,000km. It is evident, too, in air transport where liberalisation has increased traffic that is now mainly constrained by the difficulty of getting into main airports at peak times.

Another 'cross reference' from manufacturing to services has been mutual recognition. This principle, chiefly devised to encourage

Barriers / Services	Cross-border service restrictions	Restrictions on establishment	Restrictions on factor flows	Regulatory/technical barriers	Fiscal barriers	Others
Banking	✓✓ Discriminatory conditions for cross-border sale of services ✓ Restrictions on marketing and service content	✓✓ Discriminatory conditions for licences	✓✓ Capital controls	✓✓ Prudential requirements ✓ Consumer protection	✗ Tax on savings ✗ Investment income tax ✗ Death duties	
Insurance	✓✓ Discriminatory conditions for cross-border sale of services ✓ Restrictions on marketing and service content ✗ Single licence for brokers	✓✓ Discriminatory conditions for licences	✓✓ Capital controls	✓ Consumer protection conditions for sales	✗ Taxation of reserves ✗ Taxation of premiums	
Road freight transport	✓✓ Bilateral quota restrictions on the access to other EC markets ✓✓ Price restrictions	✓ Discriminatory licensing conditions	✓ Cabotage restrictions ✓✓ Recognition of diplomas	✓✓ Weights and dimensions ✓ Road safety rules ✓ Speed limiters ✓ Resting hours	✓✓ Excise duties	✓✓ Border formalities for goods
Air transport	✓✓ Bilateral restrictions on free access to other EC markets ✓ Price restrictions ✗ Slots allocation	✓✓ Exclusive rights for licensing of air carriers ✗ Ownership rules in third country bilaterals	✓ Cabotage restrictions ✓✓ Designation and capacity restrictions	✓✓ Conditions for sales ✓✓ Security and safety rules ✗ Airport charges	✓ VAT	✓ Border formalities for passengers ✓✓ Access to computer reservation systems ✓ State aids, unfair practices
Telecoms liberalised services	✓ Discriminatory conditions for access to network	✓✓ Exclusive rights on mobile, data satellite services	✓✓ Exclusive rights sell equipment	✓ Technical conditions for use of networks		✗ Fair access to networks
TV broadcasting services	✓✓ Restrictions on cross frontier broadcasting ✓ Rental and lending rights ✓ Term of copyright protection ✓ Copyright applicable to satellite and cable	✗ National licensing rules for broadcasters ✗ Media ownership restrictions ✗ National quotas on programmes		✓ Technical conditions for use of networks		✓✓ Border formalities for goods ✓ Technical barriers on products
Distribution (Fast moving consumer goods)	No restrictions	No restrictions	✓✓ Restrictions on free movement of goods		✓ VAT	✓✓ Border formalities for goods
Advertising	✗ Types of products and media ✗ Comparative advertising	No restrictions	✓ Restrictions on media	✓ Misleading advertising ✗ Content restrictions		

✓✓ Barrier effectively removed; ✓ Barrier partially removed; ✗ Remaining barrier; – Not relevant

Table 5.1 Effectiveness of single market measures in removing barriers to the free provision of services (as perceived by economic operators)

member states to mutually recognise and accept the technical differences in their goods, has also been successfully applied to services. The general approach to services has been to separate the issue of market access from that of prudential, safety and consumer protection standards. These latter aspects have been left for the home country of the service provider (whether a bank, insurer, stockbroker, airline, road haulier) to supervise. With their basic financial soundness or safety record controlled by their home authority, these companies are free to do business around the EU. And it is the mutual recognition of this 'home country' control that allows this system to work. In these service sectors, mutual recognition, in principle, gives Europe's consumers adequate protection while still giving Europe's companies plenty of access to each other's markets.

To see better how all this has worked in practice, we now take a look at several sectors.

BANKS

The single market programme gave European banks a sounder financial base and made them more competitive, more international in their operations or alliances, more diverse in the products they offer, and more explicit about the fees they charge. But it did not generally lead to a sharp downward convergence of the prices of corporate, retail and mortgage loans across the EU, as had been hoped.[1]

The price – the difference between the interest the bank charged its customer and what it had to pay on the three-month inter-bank market – of corporate loans fell slightly across the EU. As can be seen from Figure 5.1, relatively large decreases were reported in Ireland, France, Spain and, in the case of lending to large companies, in Greece and Denmark. Retail and mortgage loan prices also fell across the EU, but the price falls were less than in the corporate sector. Banks in Ireland, France and Spain reported the biggest decrease in retail loan prices, while Greece, Spain and France reported the biggest drop in mortgage prices. Those in the once-heavily regulated and restricted banking markets of the south, as well as in Ireland, were the most ready to attribute these price drops to the single market measures.

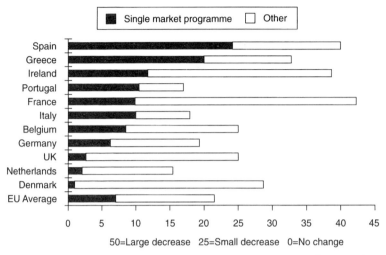

Figure 5.1 Change in loan prices by country and impact of the single market programme

Source: Postal survey

But these modest declines, unequal as they were, did nothing to push banking prices closer together across the EU. In general, loan prices converged in 1978–85, but thereafter stopped doing so. Deposit prices continued to converge from 1978 to 1995, as is shown in Figures 5.2 and 5.3, but there is no evidence that the single market programme had much to do with this.

Taking the five financial products and seven countries which the Cecchini Report examined for 1987, and comparing them with the same products in the same countries today, shows that only in the cases of credit cards and mortgages has the spread of prices narrowed over the past nine years see Tables 5.2 and 5.3.

There are several reasons for this. A major one is that EU, as well as international, regulators have obliged banks to set aside more money or profit to boost their own capital provisions against the risk of bad loans. Thus the liberalisation legislation for mutual funds (1988), banks (1989) and investment firms (1995) has been matched by the Own Funds/Solvency Directives of 1989, the Capital Adequacy Directive of 1993 and the Deposit Guarantee Scheme of 1994. Bank clients therefore gain from having at their disposal institutions that are more solid

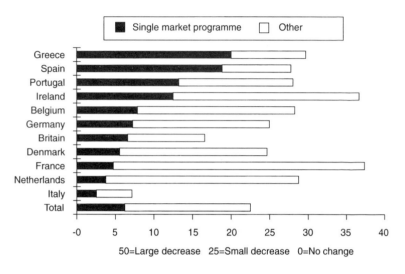

Figure 5.2 Change in deposit prices by country and impact of the single market programme

Source: Postal survey

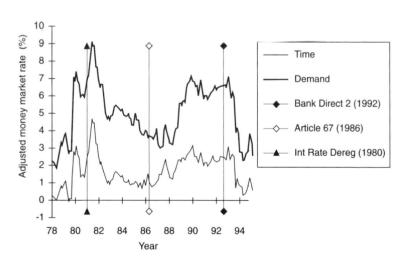

Figure 5.3 EUR-8 averages: price of demand and time deposits

Source: OECD interest rates on international and domestic markets

Product	UK	F	D	B	NL	I	E	Range[1]
Commercial loan	6875	4375	5000	4500	6750	5125	5625	2500
Credit card	61	37	84	94	75	99	66	62
Mortgage	290	653	575	480	343	350	800	510
Current cheque account	112	10	117	0	0	240	2	240
Personal equity transaction	23	9	11	14	22	10	17	13

NB: All prices are in ECUs.

Table 5.2 Cecchini Report results: the prices of five products in 1987

Source: Cecchini Report

[1] The range is simply the difference between the most and the least expensive Member States

Product	UK	F	D	B	NL	I	E	Range[1]
Commercial loan	7500	3885	2114	3755	2741	4843	6976	5386
Credit card	35	33	32	71	27	40	43	44
Mortgage	475	626	245	408	180	552	540	446
Current cheque account	4	−70	52	38	*	280	109	350
Personal equity transaction	18	51	20	13	3	3	13	48

NB: All prices are in ECUs

Table 5.3 Postal survey study results: the prices of five products in 1996

Source: Postal survey

* Figures not available
[1] The range is simply the difference between the most and the least expensive Member States

financially, though of course they might also have liked to see a decline in their bank interest bill as well.

Another reason is that banks preferred not to compete on the price of lending, especially in market conditions that were often in recent years volatile. In addition, cross-border operations may bring a bank customers of whose credit-worthiness it is less sure, and therefore it may build a higher risk premium into the price of its loans. Instead, banks have competed more on the range of their products and quality of their service. They have also become more explicit about the fees they charge customers, as required by consumer protection laws (see Chapter 9).

The single market provides most banks with what economists call 'economies of scope' – the ability to use a given network to sell a wider range of products or goods. Recent econometric research has concluded that these scope economies have been most exploited by the very biggest banks, with assets in excess of Ecus 50bn, and small to medium banks with assets of Ecus 1–10bn[2]. The same research concludes that there is still potential for economies of scale or reduced costs through an increase in market size, particularly in corporate banking, and that smaller banks in France and Germany – the two biggest national economies – are best placed to seize them.

The diversity in financial service products has, of course, broadened with the increase in cross-border banking business. The aim of the 'single passport' legislation was to avoid financial services companies from having to set up a full subsidiary in each and every EU country in which they wanted to do serious business. Nowadays, a bank can do business in a given member state either from a branch there, or directly from its home base where all the key aspects of its solvency, liquidity and risk are supervised by its home regulator. The number of branches which banks based in one EU state established in other member states rose by 58 per cent – from 308 to 487 – in the three years after 1992. Over the same period, the Commission received from third countries 43 notifications of the establishment or acquisition of subsidiaries as credit institutions.

In addition, mergers and acquisitions have increased in wholesale corporate banking, with, for instance, many of the big continental banks buying up London merchant banks. Some of the previously heavily regulated banking markets – Italy, Spain and Portugal – plus more mature but smaller markets, like the Netherlands, have seen an increase in domestic mergers that have been essentially defensive.

Banking done directly across borders has increased, particularly in off-balance sheet business and investment management, in contrast to retail banking which has seen almost no increase. Though some of the most active players in this have been German, Dutch and Irish banks, increased trade in banking services has primarily benefited southern countries, France, Belgium and the UK.

Generally then, the single market's impact on banking has been positive but not startling. Though barriers remain, the chief of which are the differing tax rates and regimes which persist around Europe, most bankers surveyed in the research have their minds fixed on the next target in European integration – monetary union. 'Without this', one of them said, 'the single market is like Hamlet without the Prince'.

TELECOMMUNICATIONS AND INFORMATION SERVICES

The liberalisation of telecommunications services stems from two landmark Directives of 1990: the Services Directive which allowed unrestricted access for service providers to the public phone network both within and between member states and the Open Network Provision Directive, which provided a framework for competition in value-added services, data transmission and ordinary voice telephony.

Rapid growth has followed. For example, the market in value added networks increased by 22 per cent in 1992 and by 26 per cent in 1993, while the expansion of the GSM mobile phone has been exponential. Since the 1990 Directives, the non-domestic providers' share of data transmission within the EU has risen from 24 to 35 per cent[3] but without squeezing out EU companies which have also seen their part of the market almost double from 12 to 23 per cent.

Growth has meant change. The liberalisation of telecommunications equipment, data and value-added telecoms services, satellite services and, from 1996, mobile communications and the use of utility-owned networks and cable TV networks adds up to a transformation of the telecoms scene. In each of these areas, the change has removed barriers to investment, led to lower prices (particularly for telephone calls between member states) and improved the quality of service for users.

Subscribers to telephone services, in particular, will have noticed that waiting times for a new phone line are shorter, faults occur less frequently and are being repaired more quickly. Compensation is often available when deadlines are not met.

The new competitive environment has resulted in a succession of recent alliances between big players in the market, such as the Unisource consortium, and link-ups such as the one between France Telecom and Deutsche Telekom, or between British Telecom and Generale des Eaux. Encouragingly, these reveal the industry's ability to meet business' demand for Europe-wide services. But this is also part of strategic positioning by the operators as they gear up to take advantage of the full liberalisation of networks and the public voice service from 1998.

Change has been for the better. Community legislation has successfully set the pace for the liberalisation process. It should continue to ensure that benefits are passed on to consumers in terms of more choice, better quality and lower priced telecommunications services. For example, the increase in competition has pushed prices downwards, most dramatically in international phone calls. Since 1990, calls from the EU to the US have fallen by 42 per cent, partly pushed down by the challenge from US 'call-back' companies. But, preparing themselves for the loss of their monopoly on ordinary telephony in 1998, EU telephone operators have also reduced the cost of long distance calls by 22 per cent. As a result, the 'gap' between the highest and lowest phone rates in the EU has narrowed from a ratio of 4:1 in 1991 to 2:1 in 1994. However, operators still struggle with some bottlenecks, such as the dearth and high price of leased lines. Tariffs on high capacity leased lines (capable of carrying data at 2Mb/s) remain on average 10 times higher than comparable lines in north America.

Liberalisation is also the 'means to the end' of bringing in a wide array of new phone-based services that are changing the way we live. Transactional services, such as phone-banking, tele-shopping, tele-medicine, distance learning, on-line news, information and entertainment services and remote-access services are becoming increasingly accessible at lower costs, thanks to the opening up of the market.

To maintain this rapid expansion, the single market in telecommunications services must work properly. In particular, no new obstacles to the creation of trans-European networks must be allowed to emerge and rob users of the full benefits. As a first step to heading off problems, new rules have recently been proposed that member states should notify Brussels (and each other) when they propose new national regulations on information services, just as they already do in the case of new draft technical rules.

GSM – a signal success.

GSM, or Global System for Mobile Communications, is arguably the world's most advanced mobile telecoms standard in the world, and is the second most widely used behind the US analogue mobile standard, AMPS. GSM has been adopted by some 140 operators in 77 countries. One of its major benefits is the ability to use the same handset throughout Europe and beyond, enabling users to roam between countries and be contactable on the same number and have all their calls billed to the same account.

Its success owes much to the beneficial effects of the single market programme.[4] For the most significant factor in its success has been the breadth of its adoption, and the subsequent impact on production volumes of equipment (leading to rapid reduction in prices as manufacturers benefit from economies of scale) and its roaming capabilities. To date, some Ecus 20bn have been invested in GSM in Europe alone, 75 per cent of this going to the five major European manufacturers.

Among several key steps along this road were:

- the European Commission's decision to reserve the 900mhz frequency range for GSM, and to defend it over a prolonged period against other claims;
- development of the standard by the European Telecommunications Standards Institute;
- rapid agreement on mutual recognition of tests and approvals of handsets;
- single market legislation introducing competition into telecoms equipment manufacture, and into telecoms services. As a result, handset prices and air-time rates have fallen sharply.

AUDIO-VISUAL SERVICES AND PRODUCTION

The seminal single market law in this area was the Television Without Frontiers (TWF) Directive of 1989, which aimed to guarantee free transmission across frontiers of broadcasts that conformed to certain standards on advertising, sponsorship and decency. In addition, a majority of transmission time was to be reserved for European programmes and 10 per cent for works made by independent producers.

The record is mixed. The TWF Directive helped some pan-European channels start up by making licensing easier, by reducing costs and encouraging a belief that a pan-European advertising market (see below) would emerge.[5] But audience penetration by pan-European channels has often been limited. In terms of trans-border broadcasting, single market measures have not, up to now, been followed by any spectacular extra-territorial expansion of territorial broadcasters. Some in fact have found it easier to enter markets by exercising their right to freedom of establishment, in most cases in joint ventures with domestic operators.

Recent Court of Justice judgments upholding the Commission's application of the Directive are expected to encourage trans-frontier activity. They clarify certain provisions and will give rise to a higher level of legal certainty, as would adoption of the Commission's proposal for a revised Directive now before the Council and European Parliament.

Indirectly, the TWF Directive appears to have encouraged the Netherlands, Portugal, and to a lesser extent Germany, Greece, Spain, Belgium and Denmark to liberalise their own domestic broadcasting markets. Competition has increased in some of these markets, with concentration – as measured in audience share – reduced in Portugal, Belgium, the Netherlands, Germany and the UK.

The rise in total hours broadcast in the EU appears to have increased the level of European television production, and the full effect of this will be felt more in the years to come. Although new broadcasters are more likely to import non-EU programmes in the early phases of their development, they will transmit more European programmes as they move into profit. The European quota provisions have had a certain impact but it has been somewhat limited by uneven application at national level. By contrast, the TWF Directive appears to have helped independent producers.

In film production, the EU's Media programme has encouraged professionals to look beyond their borders for partners and investors. But the programme is too limited by the size of its budget to do more than promote this form of personal networking. It is still noteworthy that the largest direct TV investment, by Canal Plus in France, stems from national licensing regulations there rather than from EU regulations.

Intra-EU trade in audio-visual products has increased over and above what would have been expected on the basis of relative prices and exchange rates, but there has equally been a large increase in non-EU imports, mostly from the US.

ADVERTISING

The single market's main impact on the advertising industry has come indirectly, via the effect on its clients. As companies have seen their potential markets widen across Europe, so they have sought, through advertising agencies, a more international approach to promoting their products.

As a result, there is growing standardisation of advertising campaigns, particularly in promoting products for the 'youth' and 'luxury' markets where European tastes have converged the most and where products can be sold on a single message across the EU. Even in the ordinary range of consumer goods, whose promotion is still heavily adapted to individual national markets, advertising agencies have been pressed by their clients to form themselves into international networks or alliances. A series of mergers and acquisitions has led to the creation of several Europe-based giants – among them WWP and Cordiant based in London, and Euro-RSCG and Publicis based in Paris. Some multinational groups have centralised their advertising expenditure with a single agency, though there is no clear trend here.

Cross-border trade is not a very good gauge of integration in the sector, because of the necessary proximity between agency and client. Nevertheless intra-EU trade as measured by advertising credits within the EU rose from Ecus 2bn in 1987 to Ecus 3.28bn in 1993, while extra-EU trade increased only from Ecus 1.15bn to Ecus 1.48bn over the same period.[6] General growth in advertising has been strongest in

Germany and in the relatively 'young' markets of Greece, Portugal and Spain; only Finland has seen a downturn.

EU legislation specific to the advertising industry has had a mixed impact. The first attempt to harmonise advertising rules – the 1984 directive on 'misleading advertising' – is rated as having had little effect, because member states have different views on what is 'misleading'. Germany, for example, takes a rather literal approach, believing that products must live up to all the claims made for them, while most other states accept a certain exaggeration as part of the promotion game. A 1991 Commission proposal for a Directive on 'comparative' advertising – defined as any ad which identifies similar goods or services offered by a competitor – has yet to be passed; so while comparative advertising is permitted in many member states, it is still banned in Belgium and Luxembourg. However, other Commission proposals governing advertising of baby formula, medicines, life insurance, and alcohol have been approved.

The Television Without Frontiers Directive (see previous section) contained provisions on advertising. In themselves these provisions, which for instance banned cross-border promotion of tobacco products and limited that of alcohol, would probably have restricted the volume of advertising. But this potentially restrictive effect has been more than offset by the actual growth in programming, stimulated by liberalisation at the national and EU level. The number of national and cross-border TV channels has risen steadily, from 77 in 1988 to 129 in 1993.[7] Of particular interest to advertisers is the arrival of thematic channels, devoted to a single topic (sport, culture, music, even teleshopping), especially if, like Eurosport, they reach a pan-European audience.

But generally the proliferation in the number of European media is rated as a handicap to the development of pan-European advertising. Over the 1981–91 period, the number of radio stations rose from 1,800 to 8,400, newspapers from 7,000 to 8,500 and magazines from 5,300 to 10,900.[8] This fragmentation of the media market makes it harder for agencies to mount pan-European campaigns. At the root of all this, of course, is the linguistic and cultural diversity of the EU, about which nothing can, nor should, be done. Tables 5.4 and 5.5 show the nature of the differences involved for advertising agencies and companies.

Items	Advertising agencies
Different cultural frameworks	
a) Different languages	4.16
b) Cultural differences	4.67
c) Different attitudes towards advertising	3.36
Different distribution and trade habits and systems	
a) Different product classification systems	2.77
b) Local trading and/or distribution traditions	3.26
c) Different product type customer preferences	3.34
d) Different media buying habits	2.43

(scale 1 not important, 5 very important)

Table 5.4 Cultural factors preventing advertising standardisation for advertising agencies

Source: Advertising

Items	Companies
Different cultural frameworks	
a) Different languages	3.54
b) Cultural differences	3.57
c) Different media buying habits	2.50

(scale: 1 not important, 5 very important)

Table 5.5 Cultural factors preventing advertising standardisation for companies

Source: Advertising

DISTRIBUTION

The single market has triggered a minor revolution in the trans-EU distribution of goods. It goes beyond the effects that the ending of controls and delays on the EU's internal border have had in reducing the costs, and extending the ambitions of transport companies (see next section). It has encouraged both manufacturers and retailers to tighten their control over distribution, leading to more vertical integration of distribution either by doing it themselves or by handing it over to new-style logistics companies (see Chapter 3).

This reorganisation is estimated to have reduced the costs of logistics – the whole process of transporting, warehousing and handling goods between the factory and the shop – by an average 29 per cent for some 1,000 major European companies between 1987 and 1992.[9] Over the same period, the average delay between placing an order and receiving the shipment shrank from 21 to 15 days. These gains appear to have produced a narrowing of distribution margins between producer and consumer prices in some countries (Germany and the Netherlands) but not in others (the UK and Spain).

The casualties in this reorganisation have tended to be the middlemen. General wholesalers have often been bought up by other distribution companies or eliminated from the distribution chain and forced into other activities. Likewise, the elimination of border controls has been a blow to many specialised customs clearers. But some of these companies have turned themselves into logistics specialists. The latter have become far more international, first following their customers into foreign markets and then setting up their own EU-wide systems.

Manufacturers and retailers are also adopting a more international approach. Sony, for instance, has reduced the number of its warehouses in the UK from 8 to 1 and is looking for as few as 4 for the whole of Europe, while Philips Lighting is in the process of reducing its major warehouses in Europe from 14 to 4. Warehousing and buying patterns have also changed. The single market also revived the vogue for EU-wide buying groups, particularly in food. Typically, they make only a relatively small share of their purchases together, usually for some commonly designed private-label goods or in limited products where the volume of individual purchases would be too low. As a result, these buying consortia have often evolved into training centres, or forums for the exchange of ideas or pressure groups against manufacturers.

AIR TRANSPORT

Liberalisation is opening up traffic rights on all intra-EU routes, including from April 1997 so-called 'full cabotage' or the operation of a purely domestic service in another member state. It has wrought big changes.

Scheduled passenger services increased by 3 per cent a year between 1989 and 1992 and then accelerated by 7 per cent a year in 1993–4. Further increases in capacity and traffic can be expected in 1997, when full cabotage starts. In the past, the airline industry has been very sensitive to the performance of the economy at large. Yet in the last recession to hit Europe, in the early 1990s, it managed to fare better than in the past. Indeed research has shown that, due to single market liberalisation, air traffic was actually 20 per cent *higher* in 1992–94 than could have been predicted from the industry's performance during past recessions.[10] The shipment of air cargo has also increased, made easier by the removal of internal customs controls.

The response of airlines to this more competitive environment has been varied. In larger EU countries – France, Germany and the UK – national flag carriers have acquired domestic airlines in order to prevent competitors from doing so. Direct cross border investment has increased, with British Airways buying a share of TAT in France and setting up Deutsche BA in Germany, Lufthansa investing in Austria's Lauda Air and KLM in Air UK. There is also a growing trend towards alliances. These have the effect of restricting competition in domestic markets, though they can create more competition in the broader EU market. Two such alliances with a major intra-EU impact are the linkups between Lufthansa and SAS and between Swissair, Austriair and Sabena.

The early stages of liberalisation saw some failures, such as Dan Air, German Wings or Air Europe; this led to a net loss of four EU-based carriers serving scheduled intra-EU routes in the 1989–92 period. But 1992–95 then saw a net increase of six airlines, chiefly serving low density regional routes, though a few former charter airlines (EBA in Belgium, Air Liberte in France) have opened up in competition with national flag carriers.

Some barriers to entry remain. The most important is the problem of finding new slots at big airports at peak times, where the traffic is densest but the returns best. This may prove an insuperable physical problem to further major increases in competition, although the Commission's recent proposal to the European Parliament and the Council suggesting greater transparency and liberalisation in this area should help.

Free movement of services has come a long way. A wider range of services is available to retail, public sector and industrial consumers at lower prices, particularly in newly liberalised sectors such as transport, financial services, telecommunications and broadcasting. In spite of the difficulties, price variations for identical services across the EU came down slightly from 33 per cent in 1980 to 28 per cent in 1993. So there is a perceivable trend in the right direction. The needs of the Information Society and the importance of services for the EU economy (about 70 per cent of jobs) means that this should be an area to watch for possible new measures. For such a promising 'emerging market' there must be a system of swift identification and removal of obstacles if all the benefits are to be realised.

Notes

1   Cecchini report.
2   Banking.
3   Telecom. services.
4   Telecom. equipment, Appendix A.
5   Audio-visual.
6   Advertising.
7   Advertising.
8   Advertising.
9   Study by A.T. Kearney cited in report by Coopers & Lybrand and Catholic University Leuven, on Organisation and Performance of Distribution 1996.
10 Air Transport.

Chapter 6

The 'New Look' Market

Let us now lift our gaze above the detail of individual sectors, and get a bird's eye view of how the single market programme has affected the European economy as a whole. This chapter examines the overall shape of the new European market, the increase in trade, investment and capital flows and the extent to which this greater market integration has also reduced the number of companies and price differences in certain sectors. Chapter 7 focuses on the behaviour of companies and on how they have chosen to react to greater cross-border competition. And Chapter 8 takes a look at some of the macro-economic results of all this and the impact on Europe's growth, jobs and regions.

Ideally, we should see a virtuous circle of benefits (see Figure 6.1). Single market measures should give companies some initial cost savings, increasing their efficiency and productivity. This should increase sales, and therefore profits. The profits would be ploughed back into investment and employment. Investment would give more business to makers of capital goods, while the increase of people in work with more money to spend would stimulate demand for consumer products. A rise in growth and demand would lead to a further increase in sales. And so on.

Real life, however, is rarely so simple. The first part of this cycle – the subject of this chapter – has produced economic results which are almost in line with economic theory. The removal of technical and regulatory barriers has in fact encouraged more cross-border trade, investment and concentration as stronger companies extend their reach, allying with or buying up competitors and sometimes just knocking them out of the market.

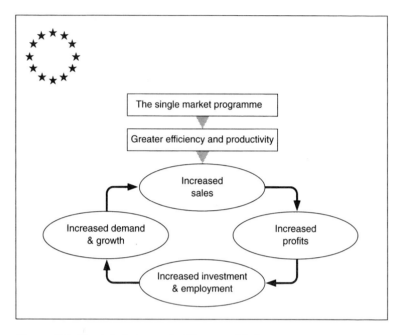

Figure 6.1 Single Market – the Virtuous Circle

But even here many extraneous factors have influenced the pace of this closer integration. Some factors pushed the single market along. Take, for instance, technical change in telecommunications. Advances in digital, cellular and satellite technology have helped telecoms equipment and mobile phone manufacturers and TV broadcasters. They have also helped to render obsolete the old monopolies of traditional national telecoms operators: new radio or satellite-based communications made it technically possible to bypass the fixed line networks of national telecom operators. Some member states were quick to recognise this obsolescence by abolishing telecoms monopolies and, thanks to the single market programme, this change is now spreading throughout Europe. Unrestricted access to Europe's phone lines has, in turn, spurred the development of a wide range of new cross-border information services.

Even more significant an influence on the pace of integration was the overall cycle of the European economy. Early expectations, for example

those outlined in the Cecchini Report, that the single market programme would give a big boost to growth, competitiveness and jobs
were based on the assumption that macro-economic forces like world
commodity prices and interest rates would push in the same direction.
The assumption was sound at the time. Oil prices fell sharply in 1985–6
and stayed low, cutting the costs of oil-consuming regions like the EU
and raising their spending power. The 1987 stock market crash proved
just a blip, but frightening enough for many EU countries to relax their
monetary policies. This provided a favourable backdrop against which
companies could confidently gear up for the challenges and opportunities of the emerging single market.

Then the economy turned downwards in 1991–2, just as many of the
single market measures were coming on stream. Demand failed to
respond to any early price cuts or quality improvements from the single
market programme, and then it slackened. This diminished the enthusiasm of companies to risk expansion. Recession made it harder for the
economy to find alternative use for those resources – companies, people,
even capital – displaced by the process of adjusting to the single market.

All this appears to have dampened the 'animal spirits' of Europe's
entrepreneurs. It is a reasonable surmise – from the evidence in trade
and investment – that after the euphoria of the build-up to '1992' they
began to take a harder look at the precise benefits from the single market
programme and to gauge their behaviour accordingly.

For instance, we have seen that, from the abolition of customs and
fiscal formalities, a manufacturer or retailer buying or selling goods
across borders has typically saved Ecus 10–30 per consignment. This is
a sizeable, but not enormous, saving, though of course its significance to
a trader depends on the volume he trades. It is big enough to encourage
a company to trade more, when times are good, but not so big as to sus-
tain its interest in cross-border commerce when times are harder. So, the
period 1985–92 saw a steady rise in the share of components which EU
companies 'sourced' or bought from other EU countries. The trend then
breaks. The post-1992 recession reversed, though not completely, this
rise in EU sourcing.[1] The cost/benefit calculation of whether or not to
trade more changes, however, when the border-related savings are in
excess of Ecus 100 per consignment, as is the case in southern European
states. Most southern states have seen a sharp and sustained rise in their

intra-EU trade.² This is especially true of Spain, even allowing for the fact that the single market programme coincided with that country's entry into the EU.

For services, the single market changes can be more significant and absolute. Some barriers to services took the form of quantitative restrictions (such as in road freight) or denial to networks or essential facilities (like computer reservation systems or landing rights and slots in the airline industry). Removal of these barriers gives a company not just a saving on the cost of shipping a good to another country, but a first chance to do business in that other country. This is bound to have a greater psychological effect. It is significant that airlines continued to expand their intra-EU services through the recent recession, despite running overall operating losses that until 1994 were increasing.³

Trade. The 1985–95 period saw a significant rise in intra-EU trade – on average an increase of 14 percentage points in exports of manufactured goods and of 7.6 percentage points in services exports. For imports, the increase is less significant – a rise of 6.7 percentage points in manufactures and of 3.1 percentage points in services. The tendency for this intra-EU trade to suffer under the impact of recession is illustrated in Figure 6.2.

The fact that member states, on average, evidently found it rather easier to sell to each other, but were, relatively speaking, slightly less inclined to buy from each other may be a poor reflection on the competitiveness and quality of EU goods and services. But overall the single market programme gave trade integration a powerful push. In a perfect world, that is one with perfect competition, maximised economies of scale and so on, the creation of the single market should have led to greater industrial specialisation by countries on the basis of their respective comparative advantage – one country exporting predominantly in cars while another relies on its main export of shirts. This would mean an increase of 'inter-industry' trade (ie one country's trade with another in a particular sector represents less than 10 per cent of that country's reciprocal trade flow in the same product).

In fact, the trade increase between the member states has been qualitatively different. It is 'intra-industry' trade which has been increasing, that is trade within the same sector where countries engage in the simultaneous import and export of similar product lines, for example, cars for

		Intra-EU export	Intra-EU import
		(share in % *vis-à-vis* world)	
EUR	1985	53.7	61.2
	1995	67.8	67.9
BLEU	1985	71.7	70.4
	1995	79.5	74.8
DK	1985	42.2	53.2
	1995	67.3	74.7
D[1]	1985	49.6	56.7
	1995	62.8	62.9
GR	1985	52.4	67.7
	1995	59.0	74.7
E	1985	51.3	61.6
	1995	69.8	77.1
F	1985	51.9	68.9
	1995	68.0	74.2
IRL	1985	68.8	72.4
	1995	82.1	73.8
I	1985	48.3	58.8
	1995	58.2	66.1
NL	1985	73.7	64.6
	1995	81.6	66.3
P	1985	63.6	70.7
	1995	81.8	84.0
UK	1985	44.7	54.4
	1995	64.4	59.3

[1] 1985: West Germany
  1995: Whole Germany

Table 6.1 Share of intra-EU trade in total trade: manufacturing

Source: Eurostat

		Intra-EU export	Intra-EU import
		(share in % *vis-à-vis* world)	
EUR	1985	42.6	46.9
	1995	50.2	50.0
BLEU	1985	62.9	63.0
	1995	69.3	62.1
DK	1985	28.6	44.3
	1995	31.3	39.2
D[1]	1985	37.4	42.9
	1995	43.6	45.7
GR	1985	43.2	44.1
	1995	50.1	49.6
E	1985	57.8	48.3
	1995	69.2	60.5
F	1985	39.4	43.4
	1995	46.0	47.5
IRL	1985	61.1	62.4
	1995	59.7	59.9
I	1985	53.2	49.7
	1995	54.0	50.6
NL	1985	53.6	51.6
	1995	59.5	54.3
P	1985	49.4	51.0
	1995	70.3	71.7
UK	1985	24.4	39.2
	1995	30.8	40.8

[1]   1985: West Germany
    1995: Whole Germany

Table 6.2 Share of intra-EU trade in total trade: services

Source: Eurostat

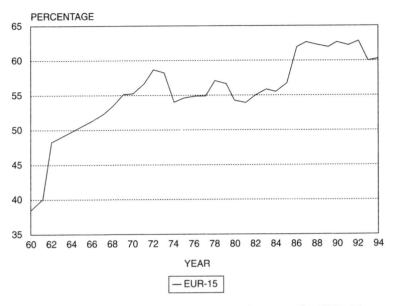

Figure 6.2 Share of intra-EU imports in total imports for EUR-15: trade in goods

Source: Ameco (DG II)

cars, or shirts for shirts which are differentiated by price and quality (expensive cars or brand-name shirts for less expensive cars or shirts). This was probably the best thing which could have happened to the EU at this time. The specialisation which would have happened in inter-industry trade would have meant some countries experienced contractions in certain sectors and expansion in others (for example, clothing vanishing in high labour cost countries and high-tech disappearing in countries with low skill levels). With intra-industry trade, the adjustments take place within firms rather than among industries. The EU economy becomes more diversified and therefore more able to stand sector-specific shocks, such as sudden increases in the price of raw materials. A shock like this would not affect one EU country more than any other – which is particularly important during the run-up to monetary union.

The rise in intra-industry has been mainly due to an increase in trade of differentiated products (from less than 35 per cent in 1985 to over 42 per cent in 1994) whilst intra-industry trade in similar products remained steady at around 20 per cent of total intra-EU trade.

In every member state, the last decade has seen a decline in the market share held by purely domestic firms. This expected result of the assault on internal trade barriers is borne out by surveys of polling, particularly in manufacturing. Some 28 per cent of manufacturers, and 12 per cent of service companies, told the Eurostat Business survey that the single market programme had contributed to their sales in other EU states.

Significantly, fears that trade within the EU would grow at the expense of trade with the outside world have not been borne out. For a wide range of industrial sectors, intra-EU imports as a share of total demand in Europe rose from an average of 20.8 per cent in 1985–88 to an average 22.9 per cent in 1989–93. This indicates that EU states *created* extra trade between themselves. But they did not do this at the expense of *diverting* trade away from the rest of the world.

As a share of final consumption, extra-EU imports have increased from 12 per cent in the period 1980–1984 to 14 per cent in the period 1989–1993.[4] In areas where the single market programme has required changes in the Community's import regime, for example, where national quotas had to be replaced by common trade arrangements, these changes have been to the benefit of producers from countries outside the EU. The EU's trade partners have benefited from the single market as much as European consumers who now have more choice at competitive prices.

Intra-EU imports, expressed this time as a ratio of total imports into Europe, stayed almost rock steady, moving only from an average of 60 per cent in 1985–88 to 60.8 per cent in 1989–93.[5]

Imports from both EU and non-EU countries have gained market share to varying degrees in EU industries and countries. For instance, in pharmaceuticals, the slice of the market held by domestic drug companies has fallen sharply in Italy, Belgium, Spain and Portugal – to the benefit of EU and non-EU companies alike. Boiler makers have lost domestic share in the UK, Italy and Spain to manufacturers from other EU states, but in Germany it is to non-EU firms that domestic manufacturers have ceded ground. In office machines and computers, domestic market shares have generally declined, to the benefit of non-European producers in France, Belgium and Ireland and of EU producers in Spain. Indeed, non-European manufacturers have actually gained in some areas, like telecommunications and data processing, which are high-tech sectors and were typified by heavy regulation and discriminatory public procurement habits.[6] This shows that deregulation has been good for everyone.

Investment. Curiously, all this increased trade has not displaced foreign investment within the EU. With the prospect of being able to sell their goods more freely around the EU, one might have imagined that many companies might be tempted to supply the new single market from a single factory, even to the extent of closing down other plants and dis-investing. In isolated cases, this has happened. But, overall, foreign direct investment – both in terms of building greenfield plants from scratch and of mergers with, or acquisitions of, existing companies – rose sharply in the late 1980s and early 1990s. Such foreign investment doubled as a share of total EU fixed asset investment, from a 2.8 per cent average in 1980–85 to 5.8 per cent in 1990–92. In 1992 the EU took in a full 50 per cent of all foreign direct investment in the world. Over half of the total foreign assets of US companies now lie in the EU.

There seem to be several reasons for this investment surge. Investors were enticed by the prospect that the single market would make local firms more competitive as suppliers, and also by the prospect of higher growth and income levels in Europe. They also appear to be attracted by the reduction in technical barriers and more open bidding for public contracts. They now know that they can decide where to build a factory within the EU more on economic or market criteria and less on the political need to be present in a particular member state to have any hope of winning a public contract in that country.

Some foreign investment, especially by non-EU companies like the Japanese, may have been drawn in by worries over possible EU threats – from dumping actions or local content rules – against direct imports. But such concerns have obviously not troubled Europeans who, in a break with the past, are now investing more in each other's countries than in the outside world.

In general, the smaller Benelux countries in the geographical core of the EU and Ireland, Spain and Portugal on its periphery were the main gainers of foreign investment coming from other EU states. The UK remained the dominant destination for investment arriving from outside the EU (with 37 per cent of all investment placed in Europe by non-European firms in 1990–93). Detailed analysis of the pattern of investment in the UK and Germany showed that the existence of the single market programme led the UK to raise its foreign direct investment in other EU states by $15bn by 1992, or 31 per cent of its overall stock of investment in the EU, while Germany increased its foreign direct investment in the EU by $6bn by 1992, or nearly 7 per cent of its total investment in Europe.

In manufacturing, there was one sector – foodstuffs – where foreign investment rose much faster than intra-EU trade. This was evidently because food producers felt they needed to be present in local markets to adapt products and marketing to local tastes. Elsewhere, investment has tended to reflect different comparative advantages, going, in northern countries, mainly into engineering, transport and machinery sectors, and, in the south, chiefly into textiles, clothing, timber and furniture.

However, the bulk of foreign investment went into services, because they are the fastest growing part of the European economy and because they are often still more easily supplied via a local branch or office than sold across borders. A significant portion of the extra UK and German investment was in financial services elsewhere in the EU. Some of this 'non-producing' investment was also made by manufacturers themselves, setting up R&D centres to track local market developments more closely, or to ensure the after-sales servicing of their goods, such as the setting up of dealerships to service cars.

Much of this investment took the form of mergers and acquisitions. These soared in the late 1980s, declined slightly in 1991–92 and then picked up again (see Figure 6.3). Some of this increase came in the number of deals made across EU borders, which in 1995 were running at three times their rate in 1986-88. However, some 60 per cent of all mergers and acquisitions still take place within a single member state. By country, France and Italy saw the biggest relative increase in mergers and acquisitions involving a company in another member state, but the absolute level of deal-making remained highest in the UK. During this period of implementing the single market, British companies were involved in no less than 58 per cent of all intra-EU mergers and acquisitions.

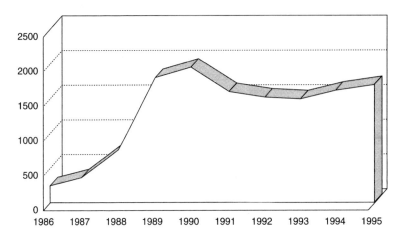

Figure 6.3 Cross-border mergers and acquisitions where a Community firm is the target (total number of events)

As we have seen in the individual cases of the UK and Germany, the single market programme was probably the major spur for companies to go on this buying spree. In addition to holding out the carrot of an expanded commercial marketplace, it has encouraged the freer and more integrated capital market that has made mergers and acquisitions easier to arrange financially.

Capital liberalisation. The removal of national controls on the movement of money – agreed in 1988, in force for most member states by 1990 and for all of them by 1994 – has paved the way for both the single market and for economic and monetary union (Emu). It abolishes restrictions which, ironically, disappeared in the early days of the Community, only to return in the 1970s when the Bretton Woods monetary system broke down and countries tried to stabilise the value of their currencies by stemming outflows.

Freedom to move money around is essential if people are to take advantage of cross-border financial services or to buy foreign shares: the right to buy an insurance policy in another country is useless if you cannot move the money to pay the premium to the company in question. Today money moves around the EU freely, or almost freely. Member states can still retain the right to restrict certain cross-border capital transactions, if they lodge reservations with the Organisation for Economic Cooperation and Development (OECD), the Paris-based group of the world's major industrialised countries to which all EU states belong.

Some ten EU states have entered such reservations against freedom of establishment and operation by foreign branches of banks and insurance companies. These apply equally to third countries as well as to other member states; none applies to other member states alone. In general, companies consider the freedom to move capital around the Community to be largely achieved. Indeed in some countries, like Greece, they rate capital liberalisation as one of the 'single market' measures with the most impact on their economy. But a few barriers to a completely free capital market remain. France and Portugal limit access to government debt or bond markets to local or selected banks, and in the UK, Germany and France foreign institutions must issue mortgage bonds through a local operation. But it is important to see this in a global context. In fact, the overall number of reservations to the OECD by member states is low (an average of 3.5 reservations). Capital moves more freely within the EU than it does between the EU and the rest of the world and there are fewer restrictions inside the EU than in the US and Japan.[7]

Concentration. Because some companies have bought each other up, while others just grew internally by extending output and sales, the result has been a smaller number of bigger players in many sectors.

Concentration, as measured by the market share of the top four suppliers, has not changed much in national markets, indicating that many companies with perhaps less of a competitive edge or with less access to the money to finance takeovers, have at least held onto their own turf. At the EU level, however, concentration had increased markedly. The share taken by the leading four manufacturers, averaged across industry as a while, rose from 20.5 to 22.8 per cent over the 1987–93 period.

But as Table 6.3 shows, this concentration ratio jumped by more than 6 percentage points from 32.9 to 38.9 per cent for sectors carrying out a lot of R&D. These industries, like telecoms and transport equipment, some processed food, and electrical machinery and appliances, are either particularly sensitive to the single market programme (through, for instance, the opening up of public procurement), or they present oppor-

Industry type:	CR4 in 1987 (%)	CR4 in 1993 (%)	Change in CR4 (87–93)
Unweighted average for total manufacturing	20.5	22.8	2.3
Conventional industries	13.2	14.4	1.2
Advertising-intensive industries	22.3	23.6	1.3
Technology-intensive industries	32.9	38.9	6.0
Industries with both high advertising and R&D expenditure	30.1	32.4	2.3

Table 6.3 Evolution of concentration at EU level (measured by share of market held by top 4 firms (CR4))

Source: EAG, Davies & Lyons (1996)

tunities for economies of scale that larger companies have clearly seized (see also Table 6.4).

The ever-narrowing spectrum of suppliers of railway rolling stock is graphically illustrated in Figure 6.4 in an industry which is in fact only a relatively moderate spender on R&D. The moves by non-EU groups like Nestlé of Switzerland to buy EU companies like Perrier and Rowntree, or Philip Morris of the US to buy Suchard, demonstrate the desire of managers to spread the high costs of advertising consumer foodstuffs across a wide range of products.

The white goods industry straddles both categories in the sense that the refrigerators and washing machines which it makes for Europe's kitchens require both R&D and promotion. It has seen considerable compression. In 1985, some 150 companies supplied 75 per cent of the European market; by 1990 15 groups controlled 80 per cent of the market; by 1995 seven groups had 86 per cent of the market.[8]

Pointing in the same direction, but far less dramatically, is the change in the car industry. The top three car manufacturers, as well as the top ten manufacturers, have seen their collective market share rise by a bit more than one per cent between 1989 and 1994. In a minority of cases, the number of EU-wide players has increased. The market for construction equipment has become more fragmented. Its top five manufacturers held 50.3 per cent in 1988, but only 42.7 per cent by 1994.[9] This sector is similar to railway rolling stock with medium level R&D

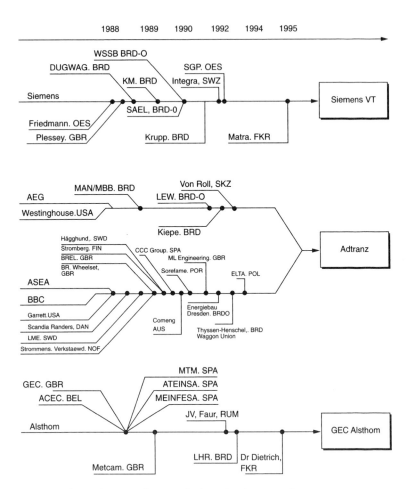

Figure 6.4 Evolution of Europe's three leading suppliers

Source: Advertising

and hardly any advertising. But there are fewer natural economies of scale in this industry where equipment is often tailored to the specifications of individual construction companies. As a result, smaller specialist firms have held their own in niches of the market, which has also seen the arrival of new entrants from Japan and Korea.

Price convergence. In a perfectly unified and perfectly competitive market, there would be a single price, or at least series of single prices per

		Growth in size		Concentration		
		% growth 1986-91 at national level		Mean national change (C4NAT)	EU level (C4EU)	
	Industry	Firm	Industry	1986-92	1987	1993
Type 1	Homogeneous goods	3.2	1.8	−0.3	12.3	16.5
Type 2a	High advertising intensity	14.3	3.5	1.3	21.1	23.5
Type 2r	High R&D intensity	−0.7	0.2	−1.9	31.6	38.9
Type 2ar	High R&D and advertising intensity	−3.9	2.3	1.3	34.8	37.2
All				−0.1	19.7	23.8

Table 6.4 Changes in size and concentration by industry type

Source: Scale economies

Notes:
1. All means are simple arithmetic averages.
2. 'Mean national' refers to the simple means of Belgium, France, Germany and the UK; for France the time period is 1985–92, for Germany it is 1987–93, and for Belgium it is 1986–91.
3. Changes in concentration ratios refer to percentage points.

sector. This has clearly not yet happened across the EU. But over the 1989–93 period, prices for a given product or service, have generally tended to converge (see model simulation figures in Chapters 4 and 5).[10] The trend has been more marked in consumer and equipment goods than for energy and construction and some services where the spread in prices actually increased. This is because consumer and equipment goods are more heavily traded across borders and are more open to competition from non-EU imports than energy, pharmaceuticals, construction and services where trade is still limited or prices sometimes regulated. Of the ten product/service categories in which there was the widest price spread in 1993, four are related to health care, reflecting national price controls in this areas.

Among consumer goods, there is a difference. The price spread is smaller for homogeneous goods like clothes or shoes where competition is mainly on price. It is wider for goods like heavy household appliances which require considerable spending on R&D and advertising (itself a barrier to entry into the market) and which are sold as much on quality and brand as price. Where lots of advertising is built into a product, like alcohol, coffee, tea and confectionery, price disparities around the EU remain (see Table 6.5).

	1980		1985		1990		1993	
	Inc. VAT	Excl. VAT	Inc. VAT	Excl. VAT	Inc. VAT	Excl. VAT	Inc. VAT	Excl. VAT
EU-6								
Consumer goods	15.9	15.7	14.2	14.2	13.5	13.4	12.4	12.6
Services	22.7	23.1	23.9	24.6	20.0	20.2	21.3	21.7
Energy	18.4	17.2	12.5	10.4	19.4	18.8	24.3	23.4
EU-9								
Consumer goods	19.9	18.8	19.1	17.7	20.3	18.5	18.0	16.6
Services	25.2	25.7	25.6	25.2	24.6	23.7	23.4	23.3
Energy	22.1	20.5	16.1	13.3	24.7	22.6	30.6	27.4
EU-12								
Consumer goods	–	–	–	–	22.8	21.8	19.6	18.4
Services	–	–	–	–	31.8	30.9	28.6	28.4
Energy	–	–	–	–	28.0	26.8	31.7	24.7
EU-15								
Consumer goods	–	–	–	–	25.9	24.6	19.6	18.4
Services	–	–	–	–	35.9	37.4	28.1	28.4
Energy	–	–	–	–	27.5	26.3	31.9	30.7

Table 6.5 Coefficients of price variation for selected groupings (based on prices incl. and excl. VAT)

Source: DRJ

Price convergence takes time. It is evident that from the above table that the longer a country has been in the EU, the nearer its prices match those of its partners. So the price differentials existing in 1993 were smaller for the original six signatories of the Treaty of Rome than for the EU of nine, smaller for the EU of nine than for the EU of 12, and so on. But the single market appears to have brought a slight acceleration of this narrowing of prices over time. Different levels and changes in VAT do not appear to have distorted general price trends, and they exert less influence on price differentials than exchange rate fluctuations. Car prices, for example, were converging until 1993 when exchange rate movements forced them apart again, particularly in countries whose currencies were more loosely linked to the exchange rate mechanism.

In theory, arbitrageurs should be able to close the price gap by trading in parallel with established distribution networks and buying goods in cheap markets and selling them in expensive ones. In practice, they still run up against considerable resistance from established distribution networks when they are dealing in products like cars or pharmaceuticals. However, fear of this parallel trade may prove a valuable discipline. A number of pharmaceutical companies claim to aim at a common launch price across Europe for their new drugs, precisely in order to avoid parallel trade, but they add that this effort is often quickly undermined by differing inflation and exchange rates so that pharmaceutical prices rapidly diverge, even before governments start imposing differing levels of control.

Notes

[1] Distribution.
[2] Trade Patterns.
[3] Air Transport.
[4] Competition.
[5] Competition.
[6] Competition.
[7] Capital Markets
[8] Price convergence.
[9] Construction.
[10] Price convergence.

Chapter 7

Competition and Competitiveness

This chapter examines the impact on companies of the single market programme, and whether and with what success they have reacted to it by improving their efficiency or by finding various ways of blunting the impact of competition.

These questions are important, because most of the gains from the single market programme were expected to come from injecting new dynamism into Europe's companies, giving them the opportunity and the incentive to gear production up for the larger market and forcing them to innovate more. For there is a handicap to be overcome. Europe still spends less of its GDP on R & D, 2 per cent, compared to 2.7 per cent in the US and Japan, and has proportionately fewer researchers and engineers, than the US and Japan, where the cost of filing and maintaining patents is also less than in Europe.[1]

That companies have felt the winds of competition more keenly is clear from various business surveys.

Table 7.1 illustrates the clear perception by a majority of businesses that they now face more rivalry from domestic, European and non-European companies in their markets, both in terms of price and the quality of goods and services. Within that overall perception, the table also shows that manufacturers detect relatively more new arrivals from other EU states in their sector than do service companies, who see more home-grown competition through national as well as EU deregulation of their sector. This squares with what we know statistically – that the EU market in manufactures is more integrated than that in services.

By sector, it appears from other polling evidence that competition is felt keenly in transport equipment, electrical machinery, textiles, food and beverages but hardly at all in non-metallic mineral products. Financial services reported themselves under competitive pressure from other EU states, while in road haulage, construction and business services the rivalry was more from domestic competitors. By country, companies on the EU periphery – mainly Irish, Spanish and Greek – reported that new competition was mostly from within the Union, while manufacturers in the two biggest national markets – Germany and France – felt themselves most exposed to competition from the outside world.

	Manufacturing			Services		
Classification	Increase	No change	Decrease	Increase	No change	Decrease
No of competitors						
Domestic firms	25	64	11	30	63	7
Other EU owned firms	39	59	2	21	77	2
Non-EU owned firms	25	74	2	9	88	2
Price competition						
Domestic firms	44	51	42	37	60	3
Other EU owned firms	41	55	4	16	81	3
Non-EU owned firms	29	67	4	9	87	3
Quality competition						
Domestic firms	33	64	3	27	69	4
Other EU owned firms	29	69	2	14	83	3
Non-EU owned firms	18	79	3	8	89	3

Table 7.1 Change in competition level on the domestic market in recent years

Profit margins. As a result of new competition, companies generally now have to strive a bit harder to make a living and to trim their profit margins. This emerges clearly from studies into price-cost margins. This can be calculated by taking the added value of a company's output, subtracting its labour costs, and then expressing the remainder as a share of its sales. The resulting price-cost margins are a good gauge of the profitability of companies and also of their market power. For instance, if a company has considerable market power – either through the quality of its products or equally through barriers that keep its competitors out or place them at a disadvantage – then it can just pass on cost increases in raw materials or labour in the form of higher prices to its customers and keep its price-cost margin high. If, on the other hand, a company's power to dictate prices to the marketplace is weakened – as one would expect from the single market programme – then it has to absorb cost increases itself, and its price-cost margin dips.

It is now clear that the single market programme has had a positive effect on competition. Efficiency gains have in fact been passed on to consumers, particularly for manufactured goods. Without this, it is estimated that profit margins would have grown by another 1 per cent *per year*. This competitive pressure on profits has been greatest in 'high tech' public procurement (see Figure 7.1 below) and sectors most sheltered from competition before 1993, such as consumer electronics, cars, textiles and clothing.

The difficulty is that, overall, price-cost margins are also heavily influenced by general swings in the economy. But if Figure 7.1 is corrected to iron out the ups and downs of the economic cycle, then the general trend becomes an annual decline of an average 0.2 per cent, or a full 2 per cent over the past decade.

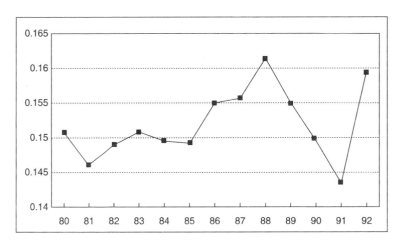

Figure 7.1 Price-cost margins, 1980–92

This trend happens to be matched by the behaviour of price-cost margins in sectors like office equipment, data processing systems, telecommunications and medical equipment. These are classically products which are bought by governments in large quantities and where barriers to free competition were highest before the single market programme. Margins here have fallen by an average 0.2 per cent a year, though from an average margin that a decade ago was as high as 14 per cent.[2] In other sectors which were plagued by technical barriers, such as electrical equipment, or sectors heavily regulated at the national level, such as pharmaceuticals and railway rolling stock, margins have shown an average decline of up to 0.15 per cent a year.

Costs. The majority of manufacturers – irrespective of their size – believe that the single market programme has had no impact on unit costs of their production, with the minority seeing a decrease almost exactly offset by those reporting an increase in unit costs. This emerges from the Business Survey (see Appendix B). But among larger manufacturers, more report lower rather than higher costs. And this trend continues until one reaches the category of firms with less than 50 employees. It is the fact that there are so many more small firms than big ones which makes the overall total look so neutral (see Table 7.2).

But there is no doubt – because they say so – that many small manufacturers have found the costs of adapting to new single market Directives quite high. These are 'one-off' costs, which involve a manager getting to grips with new EU legislation and its implications for equipment specifications, instructing his or her workforce, and redesigning the equipment. Single market legislation has not generally imposed extra recurring production costs, except where in relatively rare cases it is clearly more demanding than most of the national rules it replaces, such as EU environmental protection laws which particularly affect the chemical industry. Yet, the 'one off' cost and 'hassle' of adapting to EU measures can seem high to smaller companies. Because they are less likely to be involved in trade or use relatively few services, they have found fewer offsetting benefits flowing from the removal of border controls and deregulation of telecommunications and financial services.

Prices. There is no general trend in the level of final prices that one can firmly attribute to the single market programme. As we have seen, inflation – the rate at which prices rise – has steadied and declined in

98

	Decrease	No change	Increase
EUR-12	15	53	14
More than 1,000 employees	26	55	7
500 to 999 employees	22	57	9
200 to 499 employees	21	53	8
50 to 199 employees	16	56	13
20 to 49 employees	12	51	17

Table 7.2 Impact of the single market programme on enterprises' unit costs by size: manufacturing sector

Europe. Although the cycle of the general economy and monetary and demand-management policies in individual member states are bound to have had their own effects, simulations using data from various studies suggest that inflation rates were nevertheless 1.2 per cent lower in 1994 than they would have been without the single market programme. This figure might have been higher without the recession.

Prices in some sectors – telecoms equipment, electrical machinery, rail locomotives and wagons – have fallen dramatically, sometimes by 20–40 per cent. Some of these price falls are due to the changed behaviour of public procurement authorities who have thereby saved themselves and their taxpayers money. But recession, over-capacity (supply exceeding demand) and technological invention have also played a role. Companies' room for manoeuvre to reduce prices was, as we have seen, often constrained by their thinner profit or price-cost margins. For the sectors benefiting from improvements in distribution across EU borders stemming from the single market programme, there should probably have been more price reductions than consumers actually saw in the shops. But to the extent that distributors passed on their efficiency gains in lower charges to retailers, retailers may have often kept the savings to themselves to boost their own profit margins.

Pro-competitive behaviour. To judge from companies' own views of the single market impact on their own strategies, it has led them to focus more on buying a wider range of inputs, making their prices more competitive and developing new products and services rather than striking new cross-border alliances, setting up production plants in other EU states or buying up other companies (see Tables 7.3 and 7.4).

	Important[1]	Little or no importance	Don't know
Purchase of raw materials from other EU markets	42	45	13
Pricing	37	48	15
Penetration of EU markets	37	46	17
R&D of new products	36	47	17
More specialised products	30	52	18
Distribution networks in other EU markets	30	49	21
Pan-European labelling and packaging	30	48	22
Cooperation agreements with other companies	18	47	35
Establishment of production plants in other EU countries	16	54	30
Direct investment in other companies	16	50	34
Purchase of financial services from other EU markets	12	62	26

Table 7.3 Importance of the single market programme to the development of the strategy of enterprises in recent years: manufacturing sector

[1] Sum of 'very important' and 'quite important'.
[2] Weighted by number of employees. Percentages.

	Important[1]	Little or no importance	Don't know
Development of new products/ services	31	38	31
More specialised products/services	29	37	34
Pricing	29	39	32
Efficiency in the provision of products/services	29	37	34
Increase in cross-border provision of services	23	39	38
Establishment of operations in other EU states	19	40	41
Direct investment in other companies	16	39	45
Purchase of financial services from other EU markets	10	46	44

Table 7.4 Importance of the single market programme to the development of the strategy of enterprises in recent years: service sector

[1] Sum of 'very important' and 'quite important'.
[2] Weighted by number of employees. Percentages.

Certainly, it seems true that companies are now seeking to provide a wider range of goods and services to customers, in compensation perhaps for their reluctance to pass on any cost savings in lower prices. Likewise, a general decline in cross-border alliances fits with the logic of the single market which makes it easier for companies to trade around the EU from their home base. Indeed, the reciprocal marketing agreements which EU companies made purely within the EU declined – from 24 per cent in 1986 to 17 per cent in 1993 – as a share of the total number of their corporate alliances world-wide.[3] By contrast, they have entered into more such agreements with the rest of the world, particularly with eastern Europe of late.

A company can often make savings, or economies of scale, when by extending its production run it can reduce its average unit costs as a share of its overhead costs. It was thought that large benefits from the single market would come from companies exploiting their potential scale economies. But, generally, they have not. The implication of the Business survey is that companies say they have concentrated more on internal rather than external growth but this does not square with the recent wave of mergers and acquisitions. Nor is their claimed emphasis on internal growth consistent with evidence that most EU companies are still failing to realise the full potential of scale economies that can be made in their sector. Companies seem to be claiming that they are grasping the nettle of economies of scale when, in fact, they are going for the 'soft option' of mergers and acquisitions in order to stay profitable.

Economies of scale vary from sector to sector, depending on overheads, technology and inputs. Using engineering estimates of what constitutes a minimum efficient technical scale of production, and then comparing it with the average size of companies' actual market in relation to EU markets as a whole, research reveals that 47 out of 53 major industrial sectors in Europe still show unexploited scale economies. And this unexploited opportunity may be growing, not diminishing. In several sectors – which were thought to be at the same time particularly sensitive to single market changes and particularly rich in opportunities for scale economies, the average size of firms in terms of gross value added shrank by 11 per cent in 1981–86 and a further 13 per cent in 1986–91[4].

The reason for this puzzling trend may be the introduction of new technologies or working methods, which would reduce the importance of long production runs for these products. Ironically, for other sectors where scale economies were considered less important and which were thought to have only limited sensitivity to the single market changes, the average size of firms grew. In fact, changes in firm size seem to have more to do with the nature of competition in each industry than any direct effect of the single market programme. But, overall, the European Union has benefited from gains in efficiency and competition due to the single market programme, mostly as a result of exploiting scale advantages related to investments in marketing, brand development and R&D.

The climate for European companies' competitiveness could be enhanced by the right adjustments to company law. Cross-border mergers are still hampered by legal problems and the organisation and administration of a firm trying to operate as a truly European company is anything but simple (see Chapter 11).

Anti-competitive behaviour. This should be distinguished from *uncompetitive* behaviour. Companies can decide – usually to their detriment – not to compete or expand, rather to stay at home and count on customers staying loyal to unchanged products or services. Or companies can decide to compete on a very selective front by tailoring their products to very specific markets or abandoning some of their existing product or service range to new lower-cost suppliers and inventing new products or services. But this is, of course, competitive behaviour; it just happens not to be the full-throated corporate response to the single market that many people hoped for.

In contrast, anti-competitive behaviour takes the form of a company or industry trying to distort the rules of the game to its own advantage or to side-step or reverse single market legislation in particular and EU treaties in general. It was to be expected that some would find the winds of competition ushered in by the single market programme too chilly for comfort, and would seek to find shelter from them. In EU integration, as in nature, each action brings a reaction. Indeed, the anti-competitive reaction to the single market programme by some companies and industries, and to a lesser extent by governments through their provisions of state aid to industry, constitutes a back-handed tribute to the programme's effectiveness[5].

While it is true that the Commission has been more vigilant against anti-competitive practices in recent years, these practices may also have multiplied in reaction to the single market. Here are some examples:

- the Commission carried out investigations of alleged price-fixing cartels involving polypropylene (1986), milk quotas (1986), roofing felt (1986), flat glass (1988), thermoplastics (1988), welded steel mesh (1989), soda ash (1990), storage facilities (1992), the construction industry (1992), customs agents (1993), elevators (1993), and steel beams, cement and carton board, all in 1994;
- the Commission has also acted against moves by companies to reseal borders ostensibly opened up by the single market in cases involving pharmaceuticals, farm machinery, a number of consumer products like tennis balls, fountain pens, photo film, alcoholic drinks and cars. In the latter case, for instance, the Commission has allowed car dealers to retain their territorial rights while gradually reducing the exclusivity of their franchises and permitting individuals to trade cars in parallel with dealers;
- utilities or service providers have often tried to deny competitors access to basic assets like energy grids, telecoms and broadcasting networks or sea ports and airports. One of the aims of liberalising utilities is to crack down on this abuse.

Some forms of corporate behaviour in the single market can be ambiguous. Take joint ventures and cooperative agreements. These are generally a laudable form of cross-border integration. They can enhance competition and service, especially if they bring together complementary assets and activities, such as those between the makers of TV programmes and the owners of the cables to carry the programmes into people's sitting rooms. But joint ventures can also restrict competition, especially if the activities or assets are similar or identical. We have seen that the number of cross-border agreements involving EU companies only has declined, as cross-border trade has grown freer. But there is still a worryingly high ratio of marketing alliances between companies in exactly the same product line. In 1986–93 such agreements between 'rivals' constituted around 70 per cent of the total.

Europe has enough natural divisions and segments within its single market, created by language, culture, different national tastes, habits and loyalties, without companies artificially adding to them. Instead, the challenge for companies, large and small, is to grasp the new opportunities which continue to be offered by the single market.

Notes

1   Green Paper on Innovation, European Commission, 1995.
2   Competition.
3   Competition.
4   Competition.
5   Annual Reports on Competition, European Commission.
6   Scale Economies, 1996.

Chapter 8

Growth, Jobs and Cohesion

The acceleration in economic integration fuelled by the single market programme has made the European Union richer. But by how much?

The question is far from easy to answer – even on a theoretical level. According to economic theory, integration can boost growth in several ways. A freer flow of goods, capital and labour leads to a more efficient allocation of these resources around the EU. This may only produce a short-term increase to the level of output per head, an increase which would tail off as the European economy settles down into its new, though more efficient, equilibrium. However, in addition to producing this *static* effect, there is also the potential for integration to trigger a series of *dynamic* effects in the economy. Individuals and companies would respond to higher incomes and increased rates of return on investment by saving and investing more. A bigger, freer and more competitive market would increase the level and quality of research, development and technical innovation.

Some of these assumptions lay behind earlier estimates[1] that the single market programme – provided it was fully implemented and supported by expansive macro-economic policies – could in the medium term (technically defined as six years) boost the EU's level of GDP by somewhere between 3.2 to 5.5 per cent over that period. With only half of that time elapsed (1993 to 1995), it is now estimated that the increase in GDP is between 1 per cent and 1.5 per cent above the level that would have been achieved without the single market programme. But, theoretically at least, it is equally possible that the impact of the single market, bringing with it increased competition, might for some companies reduce the incentives to sink money into research and innovation on which they might never see a return. So, it is not possible to say that all the effects of the single market programme point in the direction of increased economic growth.

Nor, of course, is it easy to strip out all the other factors that have affected the European economy over the last decade, such as liberalisation of international trade, fluctuations in commodity prices and political changes, notably the changes taking place in the central and eastern European countries and the Commonwealth of Independent States. The incorporation of eastern Germany into the German Federal Republic boosted east German demand for goods from western Germany and other EU states, but eventually triggered inflation that led to a monetary tightening by the Bundesbank and other central banks. And for the newer members of the Union accession effects have also been extremely important.

But it is possible to try to 'control' for these factors by comparing the EU's growth record with that of its main partners, the US and Japan, which were subject to many of these broad economic trends, such as falling oil prices or the 1987 stock market crash, but not to the single market programme. (The North American Free Trade Agreement, affecting the US, only came into force in 1995.) Plotting annual average growth in terms of gross value added per head over two periods – 1975–87 and 1987–93, the EU-12 grew faster in the second period than in the first, slightly ahead of Japan's growth increase, while the US growth average fell.

The differences are small but they become larger if the change in average growth is compounded over time. So, if you look along the columns in Table 8.1 on p107 you will see that by 1993, EU-12 output per capita was 1.1 per cent higher than it would have been if the European economy had continued to expand at its pre-1987 rate, while Japanese output was only 0.2 per cent higher and US output around 2 per cent lower on the same basis. This tends to be supported by model simulations which show the same result of 1.1 per cent for 1994. This may not sound much until you equate it to Ecus – in the range of 60 bn to 80 bn. It is as if an income the size of Portugal's (with a GDP of Ecu 75 bn in 1994) had been added to the Union.

| | % pa | | pp | Cumulative impact (per cent) | | | | | | |
	1975–87	1987–93	Difference	1987	1988	1989	1990	1991	1992	1993
UK	1.82	0.38	-1.44	2.63	5.54	5.59	3.86	-0.23	-2.88	-3.00
PO	1.74	3.55	1.81	3.08	4.89	7.96	15.39	15.96	15.00	11.71
NL	0.88	2.00	1.12	-0.34	0.73	3.90	6.42	7.00	6.63	5.40
LX	2.20	2.59	0.39	-0.05	3.10	6.43	6.08	6.16	5.02	2.90
IT	2.41	1.50	-0.91	0.55	2.01	2.38	1.89	0.41	-1.46	-4.75
IR	1.73	8.60	6.87	3.97	8.46	19.00	23.78	29.88	38.78	48.05
FR	1.64	1.42	-0.22	0.18	2.56	4.66	4.49	3.16	2.18	-0.93
ES	0.85	2.40	1.55	4.66	8.72	12.40	14.98	16.18	15.85	13.61
EL	1.37	1.17	-0.20	-2.03	0.83	3.20	0.26	0.94	0.00	-2.27
DW	1.90	2.60	0.70	-0.44	0.76	1.46	4.82	6.85	5.80	1.52
DK	2.15	0.95	-1.20	-1.98	-3.02	-4.64	-5.52	-6.94	-8.02	-8.98
BE	1.59	2.12	0.53	0.32	3.29	4.81	6.17	6.52	6.49	2.90
North Italy	2.53	1.67	-0.86	0.44	2.27	2.83	2.40	0.50	-0.92	-4.42
South Italy	2.27	1.17	-1.10	0.90	1.29	1.07	0.31	0.03	-3.24	-5.91
Non-obl Spain	1.13	2.36	1.23	4.24	8.28	12.21	14.15	14.88	13.98	11.53
Obl Spain	0.64	2.45	1.81	5.03	9.02	12.34	15.52	17.15	17.34	15.26
EU12	1.72	1.78	0.06	0.84	2.98	4.31	5.25	4.75	3.59	1.06
EU6	1.85	1.96	0.11	0.03	1.74	3.04	4.30	4.38	3.29	-0.14
EU9	1.84	1.68	-0.16	0.54	2.47	3.52	4.15	3.42	2.13	-0.48
73 entrants	1.83	0.75	-1.08	2.20	4.78	5.02	3.61	0.15	-1.88	-1.67
new entrants	1.00	2.39	1.39	3.34	7.00	10.41	12.90	13.99	13.51	11.18
Obl	1.05	2.87	1.82	3.38	7.09	10.96	13.62	15.08	15.32	13.96
Japan	3.15	3.18	0.03	0.44	3.05	4.18	5.49	6.07	3.88	0.19
US	1.53	0.72	-0.81	0.58	1.99	2.16	0.98	-2.78	-2.68	-2.03

Table 8.1 Gross value added per capita growth rates after 1987 compared with 1975–87 trend

Sources: CE's E3ME database, based on Eurostat Cronos, OECD.

Employment. Caught in the recessionary cycle of the early 1990s, the EU has seen unemployment rise. But, overall, the single market programme marginally helped counter the effect of recession. Various calculations have been carried out and all of them suggest a positive net addition to jobs. Only the scale of the benefit varies – from around 300,000 to 900,000 depending on the simulation models used. More job opportunities have been accompanied by higher take-home pay of 0.4 per cent per annum as a result of the single market programme.[2] What we are seeing is the result of this positive impact partly cancelled out by negative effects such as recession and some job losses in certain sectors. In the manufacturing sector, productivity improvements and restructuring may have resulted in net job losses but the single market has more than compensated by stimulating growth and employment in services. There is some evidence that this beneficial impact is accumulating. Over the longer term, therefore, the positive effect of the single market programme on jobs may be larger yet, as rationalisation and restructuring – made all the more necessary for being long delayed – produce leaner and fitter companies and as the economy recovers from recession.

Taking manufacturing alone, the single market programme may have caused a drop in overall employment of 0.53 per cent by 1993.[3] By country, the EU measures appear to have boosted manufacturing employment by 5.11 per cent in Ireland, by 1.5 in Spain and Portugal and by 0.76 per cent in the UK and Belgium. In contrast, Germany, Luxembourg, the Netherlands and Italy are estimated to have lost, respectively, by 2.51, 2.67, 1.89 and 1.04 per cent more manufacturing jobs than they would have done if the single market programme had not been implemented. Most of the evidence suggests that low-cost economies benefited at the expense of high-cost economies, even though Belgium can hardly be called a low cost industrial producer, nor Italy a high cost one. But one of the overall results of the single market has been, as we have seen, to accelerate structural change towards services, particularly cross-border services, and here the employment picture is positive for higher cost economies.

It is scarcely easier to calculate the single market's impact on employment in individual sectors, because so many other factors are at play. Employment in pharmaceuticals, for instance, fell from its peak of

425,000 in 1992 to 397,000 in 1994.[4] But the single market measures have barely touched this sector which is still fragmented by the policies and price controls of national governments. These job losses are more the result of the global restructuring of the pharmaceutical industry in a series of mega-mergers. However, econometric studies show that the single market may have triggered job losses in plastics, rubber, industrial and agricultural machinery, while at the same time producing partially offsetting job gains in ferrous and non-ferrous metals, metal products, textiles, clothing and shoes. Employment in these last three sectors has shifted markedly from higher to lower cost economies within the EU.

In-depth research into some sectors raises the prospect of a 'J-curve' effect, in which employment dips initially but rises higher later. The telecoms equipment sector lost 150,000 jobs between 1989 and 1994. Without the single market, the loss might have been limited to 100,000, according to one study.[5] The same study, however, comments that delaying change would have severely compounded the European telecoms industry's problem of competitiveness and reduced its capacity to create new jobs over the medium term. Indeed the study predicts that, in the absence of the EU measures, Europe's telecoms equipment industry would by the year 2000 have foregone far more jobs than the 50,000 jobs it might have 'saved' short term in the early 1990s.

This industry shed 115,000 jobs over 1990–94 in public switching and transmission equipment, where competition has been ferocious and demand stagnant. But over the same period it created 28,500 new jobs, mainly in making mobile phones.[6] It is this switch of resources – the essence of restructuring – that provides a certain gage for the future. If telecoms services are included, the projections can be carried further. Assuming full liberalisation, the number of jobs in telecoms services might rise from today's level of 985,000 to 1.1m by 2005.[7] The wider multiplier effect of this on future employment and growth will be discussed in Chapter 10. Suffice it to record here that the general rule of thumb is that one new telecoms job creates 1.8 posts elsewhere in the economy.

Regional cohesion. It was a particular concern of poorer EU regions – particularly those in Ireland, Greece, Portugal and Spain – that they would lose out in the single market. More precisely, they worried that their weaker more traditional, labour-intensive industries would be unable to adjust to foreign competition through innovation and restructuring. This might mean that the 'knock-on' effect of revamping their economies would also be lost. They feared they would find themselves shoved to the technological sidelines, unable to upgrade their industry and to catch up with the richer core of the Union. These fears have proved unfounded.

Ireland, Spain and Portugal have generally benefited from the single market and have experienced convergence with the rest of the Union. The single market is an important factor in this, although it is important to bear two special factors in mind. The first is that the single market programme coincided in the case of Spain and Portugal with their entry into the EU, which itself gave their economies a powerful, and generally positive jolt. The second is that all four countries have received significant amounts of aid from the EU Structural Funds, generally devoted to infrastructure, under the regional policy of 'cohesion' designed to help their economies converge with their richer partners. It seems to have worked. In terms of GDP per head, the cohesion countries have caught up with the EU average; in fact their annual growth has been above the average over the average over the period 1987–93.

In terms of gross value per head, the less developed countries, Ireland, Greece, Portugal and Spain, have forged ahead of the EU average. They recorded below EU average annual growth of 1.05 per cent before 1987, but above average growth of 2.87 per cent after 1987. The regions which have received fund by being designated as 'Objective 1' in the jargon of EU regional policy are the whole of Ireland, Portugal, Greece, a large part of Spain, southern Italy, the new German Lander and some parts of Belgium, the Netherlands, the UK and France because their GDP is less than 75 per cent of EU GDP per head per year.

The cumulative effect of this is striking. Together the 'new entrants' – Spain, Portugal and Greece – which entered the EU in the 1980s saw their gross added value per head rise by 1993 to 11 per cent above what it would have been if they had stuck to their pre–1987 growth paths. Add Ireland in, and the result is even more spectacular – an improvement of nearly 14 per cent compared to what these four countries could have expected if their pre–1987 growth trends were simply extrapolated.

The extra increase reflects Ireland's very rapid average growth of 8.6

per cent in gross added value per head since 1987. Part of Ireland's expansion may be due to EU structural funds. But the main reasons for the relative ease with which Ireland has adapted to, and benefited from, the single market lie in its economic history and structure. It has long had a close and free-trading relationship with the UK, giving it a fairly open economy even before it joined the EU in 1973 in advance of other cohesion countries. Since the late 1970s, it has attracted a number of multinational companies. They have continued to invest in Ireland during the period of the single market programme, with a decline after 1987 in new investment projects being offset by the trend in existing foreign investors re-investing their profits in the country.

The impact on the domestic economy can be gauged from the fact that annual investment flows into Ireland averaged over 9 per cent of the country's GDP in 1990–93. This foreign investment in Ireland has been generally capital intensive and export-oriented and, as it happens, directed towards many of the sectors deemed particularly sensitive to single market measures such as telecoms, data processing and medical equipment. Spain and Portugal have also seen sizeable increases in foreign investment, but it is of a more recent vintage because their accession to the EU dates from 1986. Foreign investment takes a certain time for its beneficial effects to spill over and to promote technological progress and competitiveness in the rest of the economy. This perhaps explains the more modest increases in Spanish and Portuguese growth. But both Iberian countries have more than held their own in the single market (see Table 8.2).

| | Ratio of total annual FDI inflows to GDP | | |
	1986	1993	1990–93
Greece	0.86%	0.56%	0.64%
Spain	1.20%	1.32%	1.75%
Ireland	0.25%	7.68%	9.41%
Italy	0.05%	0.40%	0.40%
Portugal	0.65%	1.47%	2.64%
EUR-12	0.49%	0.94%	1.17%

Table 8.2 Significance of the EU's FDI inflows to GDP by Member State (1986–93)

Source: Eurostat and Commission services

The flow of foreign investment into Portugal has been almost as dramatic as that into Ireland, more than doubling its share of Portugal's total investment compared to the 1981–85 period. But the largest inflows of foreign money have gone into non-tradable sectors, such as construction or public works, or into sectors like banking, insurance and wholesale trade which are largely geared to the domestic market. However, Portugal has increased its specialisation in electrical engineering and motor vehicles – both sectors of considerable foreign investment – as well as in traditional industries like textiles and shoes.

The pattern is not dissimilar in Spain, which attracted foreign direct investment amounting to 2 per cent of its total GDP from 1986–92.[8] Since its entry into the EU, Spain has recorded growth above the EU average and has therefore slowly converged with the rest of the EU. But Spain is the largest and most diversified economy on the EU's periphery, as well as having been the most closed one before 1986. Its entry into the EU, with the consequent disappearance of tariff and quota barriers, therefore had as much effect on its economy as the regulatory changes wrought by the single market programme.

However, the combination of accession to the EU and the single market programme have forged close trade links between individual Spanish industries and their counterparts elsewhere in the EU. More than half (54 per cent) of Spain's trade with the EU in 1995 was intra-industry, either in exchanges of goods of different ranges or more commonly of different qualities. This high level of industrial interchange is typical of other larger EU states and of the overall trade pattern in the EU in recent years; it is, incidentally, also one of the reasons why we have seen competition and variety in the EU. In any case, Spain's level of intra-industry trade within the EU is now well above that of other cohesion countries, notably Greece.

Only 14 per cent of Greece's trade in 1994 with the rest of the EU was in the form of intra-industry exchanges, showing that the single market programme has not promoted any major increase in the inter-penetration of Greek industry with its counterparts.[9] This, in part, reflects the relatively modest inflows of foreign investment into the country compared with other 'cohesion' countries, and consequent poorer growth performance. Among cohesion countries, the structural shock attributable to the single market programme was largest in

Greece, which joined the EU in 1981. The impact has been all the greater because it has been unevenly spread. Three quarters of industrial output is based in just three of the country's 11 regions; and half of it is concentrated in a few sectors, such as food, textiles, and minerals extraction. Here, Greek exports still draw their competitiveness mainly from static comparative advantages like cheap labour and the availability of raw materials.

However, Greece is not the only country to have performed relatively worse since the start of the single market programme. Southern Italy or the Mezzogiorno grew, in terms of gross value added per capita, by an annual average of 1.17 per cent in 1987–93, compared to 1.67 per cent for northern Italy and compared to the 2.87 per cent average for the cohesion countries.[10] By contrast, the single market programme as well as, of course, the disbursement of EU structural aid, has seen the lessening of regional disparities in Spain, with the poorer part of the country growing faster than Catalonia and the Madrid area.

All of these trends and changes are vitally important in bringing member states together so that benefits are equally shared between businesses, consumers, workers and citizens across the EU. This can only lead to benefits by creating a strong Union less vulnerable to economic shocks and better able to keep up with the relentless pace of globalisation and technological advances.

Notes

[1] Cecchini Report.
[2] Employment & Manufacturing.
[3] Employment & Manufacturing.
[4] Pharmaceuticals.
[5] Telecom. equipment.
[6] Telecom.
[7] Information, p.3.
[8] Trade Patterns.
[9] Trade Patterns.
[10] Regional Growth.

Chapter 9

Protecting People and the Environment

The ultimate test of the single market's success is whether it benefits people. As consumers, people want easy and sure access to a wider range of cheaper goods and services. As workers, they want to be able to move to jobs if they are more plentiful over the border than at home. And as citizens, they want the right to travel and reside unhindered within the European Union.

Take **consumers** first. The single market was created not just to improve the economic environment for European business but to let Europe's consumers benefit from greater competition in the form of a wider variety of products and services, new channels of delivery and lower prices.

As every European consumer will know from his or her personal budgeting, the single market has not by itself triggered a general decline in prices. True, in some selected areas – usually where deregulation or liberalisation is occurring on a scale that surpasses that of Europe alone – prices charged to the final consumer have come down. Europeans, for instance, now pay 42 per cent less to telephone the US than they did six years ago. The cost of telephone calls within the EU has also fallen by 22 per cent. European travellers have seen the same sort of deep cuts in economy, as distinct from business, air fares. Telecommunications operators are estimated to be now able to buy their telecommunications equipment 7 per cent cheaper than they would have done if they had never agreed to set the single market programme in motion.

But as we have seen elsewhere, manufacturers and distributors have made cost savings, but they have rarely passed them on in lower prices to the final customers. The reasons vary. The territorial network of established car dealers still tends to keep out imports made potentially cheaper by currency devaluations. Governments still regulate pharmaceutical prices. And, in food, consumers themselves often shun cheaper foreign substitutes for the higher-priced local brands they know and savour.

What is on offer to Europe's consumers, however, is a more diverse range of products and services. They can step into a shop and buy a fax or a mobile phone that either did not exist before or was only sold by the monopoly national telephone company. At home, they have more cross-border satellite TV channels to watch. At banks, there are more savings plans, pension funds, mortgage and insurance schemes to choose from. The price of cars or business air travel may not be lower, but there are more car models or air flights to choose from.

With more operators offering more products and services than ever, the choice can be confusing and the risks of making the wrong purchase perhaps greater. Information has therefore become a guiding principle of European consumer protection policy. Information about the ingredients of food products, or the operating instructions of an electric drill, or the conditions of a washing machine guarantee or a life insurance premium, has become more important so that consumers can protect themselves. And if self-protection doesn't work, then consumers need more information about ways of gaining legal redress for their grievances and of alerting national or EU authorities to their problems. EU legislation on product labelling or accurate advertising is directed precisely at creating better informed and therefore better protected consumers.

But just as smaller companies are often nervous about plunging into the wider market, so many individual consumers remain wary of what they see as the pitfalls of cross-border shopping. In a revealing Eurobarometer survey in 1993 about consumers' reservations about cross-border shopping, 52 per cent of people cited the difficulty of getting goods bought abroad exchanged or repaired, 40 per cent mentioned language problems, 34 per cent had doubts about how any dispute arising from their purchase might be settled, and 31 per cent complained about the uncertainty over terms of sale.

To ease these fears, the EU has passed legislation to:

- introduce a general requirement for product safety aimed at preventing defective goods coming onto the market, backed up by measures to make manufacturers and retailers liable for any unsafe consumer product goods already in circulation. In addition, of course, there is EU safety legislation aimed at specific sectors, such as cosmetics, toys, machinery, etc. (see Chapter 3). Some of this specific legislation allows the manufacturer to put a 'CE' conformity marking on their products to show that they comply with the legal safety requirements. This mark, however, is normally only a manufacturer's claim, not an independently verified guarantee, of safety;

- protect consumers from over-persuasive salesmen on their doorsteps. This gives them time to reflect, a so-called cooling off period, in which they do not have to make any payment, and also the right to rescind a contract within a specified time limit. However, the legislation does not cover certain contracts such as insurance policies, which are these days often sold door-to-door;

- regulate distance-selling, an increasingly popular form of crossborder shopping in which the consumer does not even have to leave home. When the legislation comes into force in 1998, it will provide the buyer with a cooling off period for reflection and requires the distant seller to supply complete information. But it does not include financial services;

- prevent 'abusive' clauses in contracts which have not been explicitly negotiated between buyer and seller, and which give the seller too much power over the buyer or unfairly limits the buyer's rights;

- prevent 'misleading' advertising which exaggerates a product's benefits or conceals its risks. The 1989 Television Without Frontiers Directive has additional measures covering cross-border broadcasts. (See Chapter 5.)

As opinion surveys show, many consumers remain anxious about what happens if their cross-border purchase turns out to be defective in some way. Every EU state has legislation which gives consumers a general right in law to seek redress – quite apart from any commercial warranty which an individual manufacturer or retailer may provide. But the period in which this right can be exercised varies widely. In Germany and Austria, for instance, this general legal guarantee only lasts for 6 months after a product's purchase, while in the UK and Ireland it lasts for 6 years and in France, Belgium, Netherlands and Finland, it is theoretically indefinite. The Commission has therefore proposed that this legal guarantee last throughout the EU at least two years from the date of the good's delivery.

Much of the EU's early consumer legislation was targeted primarily at protecting buyers of goods. But the focus is increasingly switching to services, with the economic boost that the single market programme has given to this sector. Nowhere is this more apparent than in financial services. In liberalising the banking, insurance and securities industries, EU directives have already catered to consumers' interests with numerous provisions to give customers rights to redress, to withdrawal from contracts and to a minimum of information. The overwhelming number of financial institutions are also aware that their reputation for honesty and good customer service is among their most effective marketing tools in an increasingly competitive market.

But though it is early days – because some financial service directives have only just come into force – a number of problems encountered by consumers have been identified and reported to the Commission. They include:

- refusal of financial services to non-residents. Some insurance companies in one member state have either refused insurance, or given less favourable terms, to residents of certain other EU states on the ground that they constitute a higher risk than others. In another member state, certain credit institutions have, apparently for tax reasons, refused non-residents some banking services. Many consumers complain that insurance companies in another member state are reluctant to give them cover for their cars – a reluctance which the insurance companies partly explain by pointing to the extra cost of appointing fiscal and claims representatives in the country of the risk;

- difficulty in providing financial services in another member state. EU legislation allows countries to regulate the provision of financial services in order to protect the 'general good' of the public. But some countries appear to be abusing this safeguard clause to regulate foreign financial institutions, by simply making it mandatory for the foreign company to observe all of the rules of the new country in which it is operating in addition to those of the home country;

- poor quality of service and lack of information. Of particular relevance to the general functioning of the single market is the delay and expense of transferring money within the EU. A Commission survey in 1994 found that 50 per cent of banks gave no clients any written information on transferring their money abroad, that in 36 per cent of transfers, clients were double charged by both the sending and receiving bank, and that that the average total cost of making a cross-border credit transfer equivalent to Ecus 100 was Ecus 25.[1] Back in 1987, the average total charge on an Ecus 100 payment was found to be only Ecus 9. Assuming that the exchange rate risk is fairly constant, the increased cost seems to be mainly due to double charging by banks. To prevent this, the EU is in the process of adopting a measure that would speed up cross-border payments as well as reduce their cost.

Free movement of **workers** has been a right established as long ago as 1968, and the single market programme has not seen any significant increase in labour mobility. The number of EU citizens (workers plus their families) living in another EU state rose only modestly from 5.15m in 1985 to 5.48m in 1993.[2] Nor was the single market expected to produce any surge in migration within the EU. The mobile 'factor' of production, in economists' jargon, has proved to be capital rather than labour. The single market programme has seen a rise in cross-border investment so that jobs have come to people rather than people having to move to jobs, as happened in the past. This private investment, plus EU structural aid, has helped create jobs in Spain, Italy, Portugal, Greece and Ireland – all countries with a tradition of emigration. Nor has economic growth in the richer core of the Union been high enough to act as the magnet for job-seekers that it was in the 1960s.

But the single market is accelerating the shift in Europe's work force from blue to white collar workers, and in employment from technical tasks to more commercial, high-tech functions. A study into the single market programme's effect on manufacturing shows that it had almost no impact on service-related jobs, reducing them by 0.04 per cent, but hit employment among technicians by nearly 1 per cent and among those in elementary occupations by 0.65 per cent.[3] It is especially managers and highly specialised workers who tend to be transferred by their multinational companies between EU countries, with the result that their pay rates are also slowly converging across Europe in contrast to pay bargaining for the rest of the workforce which is increasingly decentralised across Europe.

Job mobility for professionals has also been made easier by an EU Directive on the recognition of higher education diplomas. This applies to regulated professions not already covered by other specific measures (as in the case of various medical professions, hairdressers, travel and insurance agents). The general system does not in fact provide for automatic acceptance of professional qualifications obtained in another member state. But it sets the host state a time limit of four months to consider an application and limits what it can demand of a would-be practitioner of a profession. The latter can be asked to provide proof of experience in his or her home state, or to complete an adaptation period or aptitude test – but only one of these three requirements.

The Directive has worked well. Only 5 per cent of applications have been turned down under the Directive, which in its first four years (1991–94) has allowed 11,000 professionals to practice in another member state. More than half these – 6,000 – were recognised by one member state alone, the UK. Of these 6,000, 3,800 were teachers. This is the result of a shortage of teachers in the UK and a surplus in countries like the Netherlands and Germany. Here at least the directive has helped match supply and demand to resolve a structural labour imbalance, even though most professionals appear to move around the EU to follow their spouses or for other personal reasons.

There is, however, one treaty freedom which affects all EU citizens, and nationals of countries outside the EU, which remains only partially fulfilled. This is the freedom to travel in the EU as if it was one's own country. Border checks on travellers, as distinct from goods, remain – except where they have been abolished by the Schengen convention, the inter-governmental agreement currently between 7 EU states, the Nordic Passport Union and the Common Travel Area between Ireland and the UK. The Commission is seeking to enlarge the achievement of this goal to the entire Union. Enlargement is desirable not only because unhindered travel within the EU is a right which opinion polls show that Europeans prize, but also because retention of controls on people carries the risk of a return to controls on their possessions or activities, even goods and services.

In addition, border controls effectively shut many non-EU nationals out of the single market. Some 12.2m non-EU nationals legally reside inside one EU state, and even if they are married or related to an EU citizen, they often require a visa to travel to another EU state. A fair number of these non-EU nationals now run their own small businesses, which they would like to see grow, perhaps branching out into another member state. But it is not easy to expand such firms when visa constraints keep the boss at home.

However, the Single Market has brought immediate benefits and a number of specific individual rights to citizens of the Union. Unfortunately, most citizens are still largely unaware of these rights and as a result in many cases fail to exercise them.

The Commission is now attempting to remedy this situation by a large-scale public information programme, called 'Citizens First!', in which people will be informed of what their rights and opportunities are under Community law relating to the single market – the right to live, study, work or look for work in another Member State, the right to travel or to buy goods and services across frontiers, the right to health care and so on. This initiative should be launched in every national language over several months and will not only help people to know and enjoy their rights but will also highlight areas where there are problems in particular countries which need to be addressed.

Last but not least, everyone has an interest in, and a right to, a clean, safe and healthy environment. In fact, Article 2 of the EC Treaty provided that the Community should have as its task, by establishing a common market, to promote *inter alia* 'a sustainable and non-inflationary growth respecting the environment'. The Community's environmental policy and the single market are therefore intertwined. At the practical level, no-one recognises the need for environmental legislation more than business. In some sectors, environmental requirements have even been an incentive for business to invest in new environmentally-friendly technologies which have also increased competitiveness. It is still too early to get a clear read-out on how the single market measures, which address environmental aspects where relevant, have actually impacted on the environment. But we do not need to wait for that.

Work continues on improving coordination between the member states' environmental measures, so that maximum protection is combined with the minimum of risk of creating new technical barriers to trade.

Looking ahead on the environment, studies undertaken estimate some important medium-term gains when single market measures in some sectors such as energy are fully implemented. The single energy market is likely to increase gas consumption, which is far less polluting than other fuels, and decrease CO_2 emissions by 105 million tonnes per year. In transport, the increase in road freight traffic (around 15 per cent for EU–15 between 1990 and 1994) means that in the absence of major improvements in vehicle fuel economy the Community will have its work cut out to achieve its CO_2 stabilisation and reduction objectives.

But all is not lost. At the same time, technological improvements made to vehicles under Community legislation, for example, in harmonised technical specifications introducing stricter emission standards, will at least in the future lead to reductions in air polluting emissions from road transport. Early estimations foresee considerable emission reductions in the regional transportation of goods. Hopefully, progress on fair and efficient transport pricing, as well as the Commission's proposed revision of the current fiscal framework for heavy goods vehicles, will result in an additional substantial reduction in emissions. The strategy to 'revamp' the Community's railways should, in the longer term, strengthen the competitive position of this environmentally more benign form of transport.

The main areas of national regulations which could benefit from closer examination are: emissions and hazards mostly covered by national legislation, for example, emissions of solvents; national eco-label schemes, which currently proliferate, in spite of progress to develop the Community eco-label, leading potentially to market distortions and customer confusion; and waste management regulations, where inadequate implementation or enforcement have resulted in different requirements for national producers.

We should expect to see the Commission taking a lead in this key area of proper integration of single market and environmental policy so as to ensure the best possible progress towards the achievement of Treaty objectives.

Notes

[1] EU Funds Transfers, COM (94) 436 final.
[2] Eurostat Migration Statistics 1995.
[3] Employment & manufacturing, table 4.17.

Chapter 10

Networks beyond the Nineties

The single market is not a static structure. The foundations are now mainly in place but some important complementary elements are still missing. In particular Europe needs to review and update its infrastructure which has up to now been organised on a national scale and according to national priorities. This means reaping the full benefit of telecoms liberalisation in spreading information technology, exploiting the potential of cheaper energy from greater competition in electricity and gas, and providing itself with a more complete and balanced transport network. These are foundations which are just as essential to the future of the single market as, for example, free movement of capital was to the recent liberalisation of financial services.

The task is, generally, not revolutionary. Where it is, the revolution has already begun. In telecoms, the EU is well down the road to liberalisation. In energy, it has taken a first step to opening up the electricity market. In transport, it is creating a more competitive market in air and road transport, but has yet to do the same for railways and, even more important, to address the separate questions of how to transport people and goods across Europe. It is therefore more a question of pursuing these revolutions to maximise the benefits.

This is especially true of *telecommunications*, because it is the carrier for information technology. The big milestone in the telecoms revolution is 1 January 1998, the date for full liberalisation of voice telephony. It is crucial that member states stick to this timetable, because only an open telecoms market can usher in the 'information' society. This will create new electronic ways of practising commerce, banking, medicine, teaching, publishing, even of conveying entertainment. Technically, these 'tele-services' can be provided just as simply across borders as within borders. Legally, however, they could be frustrated by new national regulations. Indeed, there is every reason to believe that member states will tend to regulate in very different ways, taking different views of what constitutes their general interest. Some coordination is therefore vital, which is why the Commission has proposed just such a coordinating and consultation mechanism.[1] But if – and it is a big 'if' – member states meet their telecoms liberalisation deadline and avoid obstructing the new services flowing from this, new research shows that the gains could be great.[2]

Start with the telecoms industry itself. Swift, uniform and full liberalisation in all member states could increase total revenue of telecoms operators by 25 per cent above what it would be if there was no further liberalisation beyond what exists today. By 2005, this total revenue could reach Ecus 232bn (and that in 1994 money). Much of the growth would be in non-traditional services, especially mobile telephony. If there was only patchy and delayed implementation of liberalisation, then the revenue increase would be correspondingly less, up to Ecus 214bn by 2005.

Of course, operators would find themselves having to lay out more capital expenditure, particularly new operators establishing their own networks. Under the 'rapid liberalisation scenario', such capital investment would rise by around 6.7 per cent to reach some Ecus 78bn a year by 2005, while under what might be called the 'un-synchronised' scenario for liberalisation the increase would be around 5.3 per cent a year to reach Ecus 52bn by 2005.

Jobs in the industry would increase, too. This may seem surprising in view of the job cuts that occurred at British Telecom after its privatisation a decade ago. But the current monopoly operators in Europe are now generally more efficient than BT was, and therefore have less need than BT did to shed jobs when their monopolies disappear in 1998. Lower prices, brought about by liberalisation, will also stimulate demand and thus create jobs. So, employment in telecoms – around 985,000 today – would rise to some 1.03m by 2005, but to 1.12m by the same date under the 'rapid scenario'. By contrast, if liberalisation proceeded no further than where it is today, employment might actually be 70,000 *less* than it is today.

If telecoms liberalisation proceeds apace, the resulting spread of information technology will bring about wider changes in the European economy. Some sectors , like finance, commerce and entertainment will be able to increase business by tapping markets they could not previously reach through, for instance, phone-based banking services, tele-shopping and on-line provision of video films. Others will use it to reduce their costs in, for instance, manufacturing or even health-care; tele-diagnosis could make it easier for doctors to consult specialists in hospitals.

The upshot of these wider effects, is that full liberalisation of telecoms, plus a thorough diffusion of information technology and expansion of information services, could by themselves produce a cumulative increase in overall GDP in Europe that would amount to 1.18 per cent by 2005, creating along the way some 641,000 net new jobs (see Table 10.1). The gains are more modest under the 'un-synchronised' scenario – an increase of 0.7 per cent in total EU output and an extra 263,000 net new jobs.

The **Information Society** itself has enormous potential benefits for the Community, provided that it is underpinned by single market principles of free movement and freedom of establishment. As well as liberalising telecommunications, the Community is well off the mark with its forward planning for the information society and pilot projects which aim to ensure that the essential networks will be in place to meet demand for new information society services. (It is not of course the networks themselves that are attractive to consumers but the services they deliver.)

An appropriate regulatory framework for a single market in information society services is a key element in encouraging investment in the new services it will offer and ensuring consumer confidence in this new 'virtual marketplace'. A regulatory response at EU level is required in areas such as intellectual property, privacy and media ownership. Furthermore, new single market barriers preventing the cross-border circulation of information society services must be avoided and this is why the recently proposed Transparency Directive is so essential.[3]

When it comes to the infrastructure, the success of the information society in Europe is primarily an economic rather than technological

	1995	1996	1997	1998	1999	2000	2001	2002	2003	2004	2005
Telecom employees (million)											
antimonde	0.985	0.978	0.981	0.981	0.971	0.953	0.947	0.941	0.937	0.933	0.924
unsynchronised	0.985	0.989	0.999	0.998	0.996	0.986	0.991	1.004	1.021	1.037	1.038
rapid	0.985	0.988	0.997	1.001	1.006	1.013	1.038	1.068	1.096	1.120	1.121
Capital expenditures (billion 1994 ECUs)											
antimonde	40.5	41.8	42.9	44.0	45.0	46.1	47.2	48.3	49.4	50.5	51.7
unsynchronised	40.5	42.0	43.6	47.0	50.9	54.1	57.6	60.5	63.3	66.1	68.1
rapid	40.4	43.4	47.0	52.8	59.1	63.6	68.0	71.5	73.7	76.1	77.6
Telecom value added (billion 1994 ECUs)											
antimonde	75.5	76.1	76.6	76.8	77.1	77.3	77.6	77.8	78.1	78.4	78.7
unsynchronised	75.5	76.1	77.1	78.8	81.6	84.9	87.1	89.4	93.2	97.3	101.6
rapid	75.5	79.1	83.2	86.3	90.8	94.6	98.1	101.6	106.1	111.1	116.2
Telecom revenues (billion 1994 ECUs)											
antimonde	134	140	147	155	161	165	170	175	179	183	185
unsynchronised	134	142	152	161	168	175	183	192	201	209	214
rapid	134	143	153	163	172	181	192	205	216	227	233

Table 10.1 Annual EU-wide telecom sector projections

issue – the technology exists, whereas, so far, the investment does not. Only the scale of the single market is sufficient to justify and attract the finance necessary for high performance trans-European networks. They must be Europe-wide: first, because national markets are mostly too small to fund the infrastructure costs of the most efficient broadband networks and second, because many information society services are likely to be aimed at niche markets which in any one member state could prove to be too small. An added bonus could be that the speed and capacity of these new services in combining text, visual and voice communications may allow them to break through language barriers. That could do a lot for the 'entente Européenne'.

As current initiatives on the part of governments, business and European Institutions proceed, the big question that remains largely unanswered is whether the Council of Ministers and the European Parliament will want to play ball as far as the Commission's efforts are concerned. There appears to be a general political consensus at all levels to ensure that Europe is well placed and indeed at the leading edge of developments in the information society.

Electricity is the most versatile form of energy and its price is vital to Europe's economy and competitiveness. However, electricity prices vary widely across the EU. In 1995, prices to the residential sector varied by almost 50 per cent, prices to industrial consumers by over 70 per cent, and prices to commercial users by more than 100 per cent.[4] This is largely the result of lack of competition.

The electricity industry is often considered a 'natural monopoly'. This is certainly true of its transmission. To cover Europe with competing lines of power pylons would make no economic, let alone environmental, sense. But its monopolistic character has often extended into power generation – an area which is not naturally monopolistic – through vertically-integrated companies which combine the generation of electricity with its distribution.

Important steps were made in the early 1990s in the form of European Union Directives on the transit of electricity between specified grids for industrial end users and on price transparency. But efforts at market liberalisation are only now coming to fruition. Member states agreed on a Directive about common rules for the single market in electricity on 25 July 1996 and the Directive was later presented to the

European Parliament. Member states have agreed to open up a percentage of their national market to progressive levels of competition. This portion of the market must include all end-customers who consume more than 100 GWh per annum. It must also include distribution companies designated as eligible to supply the volume of electricity consumed by their customers. Beyond these requirements, member states are free to define customers eligible to take part in the market opening, which is due to be phased in gradually, over six years, starting in 1997 (subject to approval by the European Parliament).

It is estimated that the share of the total electricity market thus opened to potential competition will be around 22 per cent at the start, and around 33 per cent within six years. The Directive will then continue to apply for a further three years. Already, member states have recognised in this Directive the need for further liberalisation. They have undertaken to examine the possibility of further market opening which would be effective 9 years after the Directive's entry into force.

New research, based on the assumption of a 30 per cent opening of the electricity market, shows that this measure should produce savings for consumers of around Ecus 4–6bn a year,[5] compared to what they could expect if the market stayed unchanged. These savings would be split between large industrial consumers who can expect a 5–11 per cent decrease in their power bills and a smaller decrease of 2–4 per cent for residential consumers. The majority of the savings will come from lower construction and operating costs for generating plant, and from the likelihood that cheaper forms of generation, especially from gas, will be favoured. If, at some later date, the EU were to move to a completely free electricity market, savings to consumers would double, to Ecus 10–12bn a year.

Furthest from realisation, but most significant in macro-economic terms, is an integrated and balanced **transport** infrastructure and policy for the EU. There are two pressing problems. One is action on the 14 Trans-European Networks (TENs) projects proposed by the Commission, which still await agreement on their funding. More than half of these TENs projects concern improving old rail links or building new ones. The other 'missing link' is a proper policy for Europe's railways. The latter has become the Cinderella of European transport, squeezed by its two sisters – road and air transport – which have been able, through liberalisation, to increase efficiency and range and quality of service. In a White Paper in July 1996 the Commission has called for action to clarify the finances of railways, open them up to more cross-border competition and to modernise their infrastructure.

The message of new research is that really significant gains for Europe's transport users can only come from combining policy and infrastructure improvements. This emerges from a complex study into EU transport problems.[6] The bottom line of this study is that the EU could save transport users, and earn transport operators, a combined total of Ecus 138bn a year by 2005 in terms of money, time, and reductions in other indirect costs like inflexibility.[7] But such a big saving can only be reached if a whole building block of measures is carried out:

- under a 'partial integration' scenario, assuming that the TENs projects were started and completed by 2005 with little change in policies, the combined savings in so-called dis-utility costs (both direct and indirect transport costs) would amount to a mere Ecus 10bn a year. The reason is that while infrastructure improvements can have a major local impact, they produce macro-economic gains that are minor compared with policy changes affecting the entire EU;

- things change under a 'full integration' scenario. This presupposes that to the TENs infrastructure improvements is added a whole series of policy measures, including price changes. Cost savings would go chiefly to passengers, mainly through accelerated air transport liberalisation and still cheaper air fares. Time savings would come from emptier roads, most of which would have tolls, increased use of air travel and further elimination of border delays. Higher road operating costs (diesel tax, tolls) would force freight that was cost rather than time-sensitive onto other forms of transport such as inland waterways. Total direct and indirect savings would amount to Ecus 95bn;

- on top of this last set of policies might be added a policy of 'congestion charging' to discourage use of all busy roads at peak times. This would dramatically raise the road operator revenues. How much users gained in practice would depend on how these revenues were recycled;

- a last improvement would be a determined effort to improve the quality of rail service to attract both passengers and freight. Only if this ultimate step were taken would total potential savings to transport users' approach the figure of Ecus 138bn a year. Yet, it is a prize worth considering, for it might amount to 1–1.5 per cent of EU output by 2005 (see Table 10.2).

	Cost savings	Time savings	Total cost & time savings	Total savings (including other indirect costs)
Partial integration (PI)				
Passenger savings	–3,914	3,195	–719	2,854
Freight savings	4,569	–1,649	2,920	5,980
Operator revenue	1,434		1,434	1,434
Total	**2,089**	**1,546**	**3,635**	**10,268**
Full integration (FI)				
Passenger savings	44,280	23,377	67,657	77,708
Freight savings	–6,999	–10,259	–17,258	–1,367
Operator revenue	16,126		16,126	16,126
Total	**53,407**	**13,118**	**66,525**	**92,467**
Congestion charging (CC) (Based on FI)				
Passenger savings	102	37,953	38,055	51,330
Freight savings	–12,302	–13,215	–25,517	–5,021
Operator revenue	73,012		73,012	73,012
Total	**60,812**	**24,738**	**85,550**	**119,321**
Rail Service Quality (RQI) (Based on CC)				
Passenger savings	439	39,903	40,342	53,262
Freight savings	–12,661	–12,229	–24,890	–3,412
Operator revenue	79,115		79,115	79,115
Total	**66,893**	**27,674**	**94,567**	**128,965**

Table 10.2 Ranking of overall benefits of each scenario as compared with the 2005 Base (annual savings against 2005 Base – Million ECU 91)

Notes: Transport study see Appendix C

Notes

[1] Proposed Directive for a Transparency Mechanism for Information Society Services, COM(96)392 final of 30.8.96.
[2] Information.
[3] Proposed Directive for a Transparency Mechanism for Information Society Services, COM(96)392 final of 30.8.96.
[4] Energy.
[5] Energy.
[6] Transport.
[7] Transport.

Chapter 11

Looking To The Future

It is an exaggeration to liken the job of completing the single market to that of Sisyphus, the ancient Greek condemned to roll a boulder uphill only to have it forever rolling back. But it is true that the EU's very success in removing so many barriers to its single market, and embarking on new initiatives in sensitive areas like energy, inevitably casts more light on the obstacles that remain. So this chapter looks at the unfinished business of the single market and what needs to be done to tackle the outstanding problems and take up new challenges.

Some of the problems are old ones, like tax. Business has long clamoured for more simple and consistent tax conditions and an end to distortions resulting from different national tax regimes that prevent companies conducting their business as a single, Union-wide operation. But Commission proposals to try to achieve this have so often foundered on the opposition of member states, whose unanimous approval is required for any fiscal change. As a result, no fewer than 18 tax proposals still lie un-agreed on the table of the Council of Ministers, even though over the years the Commission has withdrawn some 30 other proposals when they gathered too much dust.

Yet the run-up to Economic and Monetary Union makes it all the more striking that the same member states which are making efforts to end exchange rate distortions once and for all through a single currency cannot seem to bring themselves to make a similar effort to end tax distortions throughout the EU. This is important; the most significant obstacles are cross-sectoral and not confined to any one area. The lack of harmonisation itself is not a problem – differences between national systems are fine, as long as they are neither discriminatory nor distortionary.

There are four clear taxation policy needs for the single market:

- to end all forms of double taxation on cross-border income flows. Business complains about discriminatory tax treatment of permanent establishments compared to domestic companies, the absence of a common system for consolidating losses within groups and the levying of withholding taxes on cross-border interest and royalty payments. UNICE, the European employers' organisation, complains of the distortions these problems create.[1] Withholding taxes on interest tends to favour local financing, it notes, even though this may be more costly to the company concerned;

- to remove cross-border anomalies in personal tax. At present, there is the perverse situation that a frontier worker who resides in one EU state but works in another is often denied various forms of tax relief, while another form of cross-border activity – putting savings in a foreign bank – is often treated more advantageously. On investment income a non-resident can generally escape paying tax but a resident cannot;

- to convert the Value Added Tax system so that the tax is paid in the country where the product originates, just as happens inside a member state. There is strong business support for such a switch, which would be much simpler to apply (see Chapter 3). The Commission has recently proposed a work programme which could involve removing any distinction between domestic and intra-EU transactions over the next 3 years;

- to remove distortions in capital movements arising from differences in the Income Taxation of investment earnings.

But the problem of taxation is only one of the pieces of unfinished business which the European Union still has to address as far as the single market is concerned.

According to the Commission, in its latest report on the impact and effectiveness of the single market, issued in October 1996, the action needed to put the single market into top gear falls into four main areas: effective application and enforcement of Community law; getting rid of unnecessary 'red tape' at national and EU level; filling a few important gaps still missing since 1985; and complementary action at Community level without which the single market would be forever hamstrung, the first and foremost being a single currency. We will look at each of them in turn.

ENFORCEMENT OF THE RULES

Proper enforcement of common rules across the entire single market is a major priority. The removal of internal frontiers has completely altered the environment in which enforcement takes place. Products and services which are only controlled (or not controlled) in their country of origin can be marketed anywhere in the Union. This issue of enforcement is widely seen as a problem by businesses and individuals who suffer from delays in implementation of the law in some member states and variations in its interpretation and enforcement from one member state to another. To play fairly there must be one set of rules to which all players should not only subscribe but be seen to subscribe. Each member state's benefit from the single market depends on the level of commitment and action of the other fourteen countries, so openness is essential.

Enforcement is also important for ensuring equivalent levels of safety and security throughout the Union. This may mean that some changes are necessary in the administrative and even judicial culture in each member state. The Commission is the guardian of the Treaty and in its role of 'referee' we should expect to see it suggesting a stepping-up of monitoring and surveillance of compliance with Community rules.

However, there is plenty of room for an innovative approach. Improving the national collection of statistical data (especially on services) and greater use of the Commission's network of Euro-Info Centres could make monitoring the operation of the single market easier. Member states could talk to each other more openly about enforcement and be ready to exchange detailed information about their enforcement structures, procedures and problems. 'Audits' of national enforcement measures would help to establish a high level of confidence between enforcement agencies in the member states – to the benefit, of course, of business and consumers. Scientific and technical expertise will need to be better mobilised to give advice on how single market rules should be adapted to take account of new circumstances. Complaints about unfair or ineffective enforcement of the rules will need to be followed up more quickly.

GETTING RID OF RED TAPE

The earlier chapters of this book have shown that the single market initiative has already removed a significant amount of red tape by replacing 15 different sets of national rules by a single set of Community rules. But it is clear that much more can be done to reduce the burden of regulation to the minimum required to ensure the public good.

When it comes to getting rid of this red tape, the situation calls for concerted action. Some national legislation untouched by the single market programme is still a significant and perhaps now unnecessary barrier to market access and cross-border operations. There needs to be a way to highlight such legislation and simplify it where possible.

More could be done, for example, by drawing up a register of national measures which have the effect of fragmenting the market so that such measures could be reviewed, or looking at the possible reduction of administrative burdens arising from member states' regulations, especially measures which make it difficult for new companies to start up. Regular exchanges between member states of information from reviews of national legislation, in terms of how it can be reduced or made less costly for business (or whether it is needed at all), would be a valuable way of helping national authorities to learn from each other.

In addition, there are long-standing national rules which can deter companies from entering a given market or expanding once they are in it. The pharmaceutical sector remains rigged by governments who impose different levels of price controls. Likewise, there are widely varying national rules on how long shops may stay open, or the extent to which supermarkets can expand. These have an economic effect; short opening hours, for instance, increase a retailer's fixed overhead costs. It has never been the EU's aim to harmonise such rules. But critics who complain that European business is still over-regulated – and it probably is – should bear in mind that much of the over-regulation now exists at the national, not the EU level.

As far as simplifying Community rules is concerned, a start has already been made through the Simpler Legislation for the Internal Market or, appropriately, 'SLIM' initiative. This is developing ideas to simplify Community Directives and where necessary the national rules which implement them. A report on the first four areas (INTRASTAT, construction products, ornamental plants and recognition of diplomas) was presented to the Council in November 1996. But this is only a start and the scope of the exercise needs to be extended.

COMPLETING THE LEGAL FRAMEWORK

Then there is the challenge of completing the single market so that all its benefits can be delivered. It is a great disappointment that 11 years after the 1985 White Paper some elements of the original blueprint have yet to get off the drawing-board. Developments in society since then also mean that it makes sense to have common rules in some new areas. These gaps in single market legislation are critical to furthering growth, competitiveness and jobs and to ensuring that people can easily exercise their rights.

For example, there is the lack of a legal framework for the removal of border controls on persons. The Council has three proposals on this issue before it. And the implementation of existing rules on the right to move and reside freely within the Community and the acquisition and preservation of entitlements to social benefits both need to be improved.

In company law, business continues to suffer from being unable to free itself from 15 sets of national 'red tape'. Problems which have been around for a long time include the legal problems involved in cross-border mergers and the mass of separate national regulations governing companies and their operations. Two unadopted proposals, the 10th Company Law Directive (which would provide the necessary legal framework for cross-border mergers) and the European Company Statute would allow companies to reap considerable cost savings through reorganisation. The European Company Statute would save firms the time and expense of having to register as separate companies all over the EU, together with the additional filing and disclosure obligations involved. The 13th Directive on takeovers would guarantee minimum standards of protection for shareholders where a change of control occurs, as well as a more secure legal framework in which barriers to takeovers might be addressed.

Benefits would also accrue to business and consumers if some ambiguous or over-complex single market legislation could be rationalised. Construction products and financial services pose two of the biggest headaches. Others are probably still 'at large' but so far unidentified.

The problems of taxation have already been referred to above.

Other challenges to the single market are newer. They must be met if we are to keep the single market up to the mark for the European and world economies of the 21st century.

Let's take new technologies first. As we have seen, the needs of the Information Society will be ignored at the EU's peril. But as national authorities seek to establish rules for information technology-based services, they may inadvertently re-fragment the single market. The left hand must let the right hand know what it is doing. More work is needed to coordinate the legislative measures that will determine how the new networks can operate or how the principle of 'mutual recognition' of national rules and services could be extended to these emerging markets. Biotechnology is another key technology affecting the development of a wide range of new products in the fields of medicine, agricultural products and foodstuffs. Without common science-based legislation compatible with the single market, European research and exploitation of its results will be discouraged – to the advantage of competitors.

The services sector contains about 70 per cent of the EU's jobs, but it is also the area where the single market legislation has in places worked least effectively. Additional action may be needed to overcome obstacles to the cross-border provision of services or establishment. For example, as we have seen in Chapter 5, financial services has some way to go before it is possible to speak of a single market. This is partly due to the failure of some member states to implement the relevant Directives, especially in insurance, and to do so correctly and on time. But the scope of the law needs to be extended to provide a single authorisation procedure for insurance intermediaries. In other cases there are difficulties with the interpretation of the legislation which hampers cross-border provision of services or establishment; for example, national rules have sometimes been used ostensibly to protect the 'general good' but the result has been an unnecessary and unworkable burden for operators from other member states. The Commission has already declared its intention to remedy such loopholes in the legislation.

On the other hand, services is also the area with most potential for extending the single market. The liberalisation of the gas market, building on the progress made so far to open up the electricity market, will be necessary in order to achieve the single energy market.

The objective of environmental protection, laudable in itself, has given rise to some new barriers. Uncoordinated technical legislation aimed at protecting the environment and consumers is frequently seen by business as a complication in the single market and a reason for a greater degree of harmonisation of the rules. In some cases, the problem may be linked to shortcomings in existing EU legislation as, for example, in waste recovery, where there is little restriction on the type of measures that member states can adopt. In others, Community rules have been overtaken by additional, more stringent, specifications at national level. Such differentiation has a significant impact on smaller companies seeking to enter new markets. Although some of these measures can be justified by Treaty provisions, they may sometimes be out of proportion to their objectives. Invocation of the subsidiarity principle and recourse to Article 100a(4) to justify the maintenance of national environmental protection measures also worries some sectors, particularly chemicals, although to date recourse to Article 100a(4) has been limited to a handful of cases with limited trade effects.

In this and other areas, a Community framework may in many cases be the best guarantee that action taken has maximum impact and strikes the right balance between the single market and appropriate objectives.

COMPLEMENTARY ACTION AT COMMUNITY LEVEL

A common legal framework alone is not enough to deliver a properly working single market. Other policies will have to come into play to breath life into the body that has been created. Two of the most important are to give the single market a single currency to work with and to extend it eastward as central and east European countries negotiate to join the Union.

A SINGLE CURRENCY

Research for this review has supported, and in some cases strengthened, the case for economic and monetary union (EMU). One constant is the transaction cost of moving money in and out of Europe's multiple currencies. In absolute terms, it has risen, from Ecus 33.1bn in 1986 to Ecus 58.1bn in 1995.[2] But this is no greater a share of GDP in 1995 (0.96 per cent) than it was in 1986 (0.93 per cent). However, the relatively disappointing impact that the single market has had in terms of bringing national price levels together (see Chapter 6) is probably partly due to the way prices differences across Europe are obscured by being expressed in different currencies. The clear expression of prices in a single currency would expose the price mark-ups made by companies in some markets, while at the same time whetting the appetite of consumers to go hunting for cross-border bargains. The arrival of the Euro would consolidate and increase the efficiency of the single market.

Exchange rate fluctuations, which succeeded the period of monetary calm in 1987–92, have shaken the single market but in so doing have also strengthened the case for Emu. The overall judgement of the Commission, confirmed by other international institutions, is that the currency turmoil of 1992–93 may have led, by 1995, to a slowdown in growth of the order of 0.25–0.5 of a percentage point.[3] The further monetary fluctuations that occurred in the spring of 1995 are estimated to have had an even bigger effect on growth, perhaps reducing overall output in the EU in 1995–96 by as much as up to 2 percentage points. This second bout of currency disruption came just as the EU economy seemed to be recovering from recession and therefore shook investors' plans all the more.

The effect of these fluctuations on national economies has been varied and sometimes unpredictable. Not all countries whose currencies have appreciated since 1992-93 have, in fact, seen their international competitiveness or trade balance suffer. Nonetheless, this monetary instability has brought calls by some countries to be allowed to increase subsidies and safeguard measures to protect themselves from what they see as a threat from partners' devaluations. The introduction of a single currency would obviously remove any justification for such protectionism, and act as the 'guarantor' of the single market.

OTHER COMMUNITY POLICIES

As we have also seen, the single market is a fulcrum which can be used to create jobs. This can be given added momentum if the Community supports national training and active labour policies, for example, through the European Social Fund. Competition policy may need to be reconsidered so as to fine-tune and streamline the Community's guidelines on state aids. Tax policy has recently been the subject of a recent Commission report on the need for a coherent overall Community tax policy, taking into account the views of the representatives of European Finance Ministers. Together with action on enterprise policy aimed at helping small and medium-sized enterprises (SMEs) through the Multi-annual SME Programme, consumer policy, Trans-European Networks, and the progressive development of Community Research, Development and Technology policy (which contributes the scientific knowledge necessary for the implementation of the single market in a number of fields) this adds up to a fair-sized list of support measures for the single market.

Further down the road lies enlargement of the Union, and with it, of the single market. Central and European countries have already begun trying to align their legislation with that of the single market. This will be far from easy. As we have seen from this review, the single market is a market in motion, and therefore to some extent, applicants to join the Union are chasing a moving target. On the other hand, the early adoption of single market measures can help the acceding countries to get into a position from which they can quickly exploit the advantages of the single market after their accession. The Union has already committed staff to giving them technical assistance for this task, as well as the more difficult one of acquiring the know-how to put the rules into practice.

THE SINGLE MARKET AND TOMORROW'S EUROPE

So where does all this leave us? The single market remains politically centre-stage as a key instrument through which the priorities of the Union can be delivered. Nothing else approaching its dimensions or its dynamism has yet come onto the scene to steal the show.

Jobs remain a major challenge. Already there are signs that even during a severe recession the single market is making a positive contribution to overall employment levels in the Union. A more favourable economic climate augurs well for better results in the future.

The Community is also facing the challenge of increasingly rapid globalisation – many of the world's markets are becoming one huge trading centre. The single market is by far the most extensive and successful example of eliminating barriers between national markets. If the momentum is sustained, both in maintaining the market framework in tip-top running order and a business community which is in step with it, the Community will be well placed to influence and exploit the wider opportunities which globalisation will offer. The extension of the single market to other services will accelerate this trend, as will the effects of the full entry into force of legislation already in place.

The achievement of Emu will contribute to the efficient operation of the single market by eliminating transactions costs of almost 1 per cent of GDP and the exchange risks currently involved in cross-border payments. It will also make the wasteful allocation of resources needed to manage these problems a thing of the past. By promoting convergence and a more homogeneous economic environment, the single market will contribute to the right conditions for the success of Emu.

The EU's commitment to developing its relationship with the central and eastern European countries (through the Europe Agreements and through the negotiations for enlargement) places the takeover of the 'acquis' (the body of legislation, policies and understandings which underpins the single market) squarely on the agenda. How this will work in practice will be strongly influenced by how much these countries perceive it as comprehensive and fully operational, based not only on a complete and coherent legal framework but on the institutions, structures and practices to support it.

As the European Union approaches the beginning of a new century, we can look forward to ever closer economic integration, for which the single market will be the most important means of unity and cooperation, and to increasingly more fruitful relations with its trading partners in the wider world.

Notes

[1]   UNICE statement, 8 July 1996.
[2]   Currency costs.
[3]   Monetary Fluctuations and the Single Market, Commission statement, 31/10/95.

Appendix A

The Structure of Research

In response to the Council Resolution to report in 1996 on the effectiveness and impact of the Single Market Programme (SMP) the Commission launched a series of independent research studies to assess the impact of the SMP on both specific business sectors and across the economy as a whole. To ensure the independence and objectivity of the work, the background research was carried out by contracted parties, operating only subject to quality control by Commission services. In addition, a panel of independent academic experts was appointed to ensure that sound methods of analysis were employed. The structure of the study programme is outlined below.

The research programme was designed to elicit information on what in fact had happened in the market place as a result of the implementation of the SMP rather than to validate previous research into the effects of the single market. It should therefore not be seen as a 'Cecchini Mark 2' report.

The research consists of 38 studies, accompanied by a wide-ranging business survey.

To measure the effectiveness of the SMP a common methodological approach was established. A 'bottom-up' approach was followed to assess the difference that the single market legislation has made to specific chosen economic sectors covering both manufacturing and service industries. This was complemented by a cross-sectoral analysis at the macro level in order to measure the single market impact on trade, investment, competition, and aggregate and regional levels and to assess the effectiveness of the dismantling of barriers to the free movement of capital, goods and services.

Half of these 38 studies are sectoral while the rest adopt a 'horizontal' approach to the measurement of the impact of the single market. It would have been impossible to carry out individual studies on all sectors of the economy and choices had to be made on the basis of the economic significance of the sector and relevance to the operation of the single market. The combination of examination at both the sectoral and horizontal level should mean that no aspect of the single market impact has been overlooked

From the information gathered at the micro and macro levels a picture emerges of how the SMP has translated into broader effects in the Community and national economies, shedding light on the mechanisms through which SMP effects have permeated economic activity. The research does not simply focus on the consequences of liberalisation and harmonisation measures but inevitably throws the spotlight on to other Community and national policies which influence the business dynamics and adjustment mechanisms liberalised by the single market. Foremost amongst these policies are monetary integration, the regional impact of the single market, competitiveness and employment, competition, the environment and the promotion of consumer interests.

However, the results derived from the research undertaken in the framework of this exercise need to be qualified. Measuring what in effect is the impact of the legislative programme on the basis of economic criteria is not as straightforward as it might appear. Assumptions had to be made regarding:

- what the economy would really look like in the absence of the single market in order to draw meaningful comparisons;
- how the late transposition or implementation of single market measures may have affected the response economic operators; and
- how the interaction of the SMP with other factors that have influenced the economy in the same period may have amplified or dampened the single market effect.

This research amounts to the first extensive ex-post analysis of what has been happening to the European economy as a result of the SMP. In terms of economic impact the conclusion is positive and encouraging. The Community needs to build on its success and iron out the remaining practical difficulties that inhibit the full potential of the single market from being exploited. The debate that will ensue from this research programme and the accompanying Commission report are timely and should inform the debate about priorities for the future development of the single market.

The research was funded by the European Commission and coordinated under the direction of Mario Monti by the following Steering Committee:

Directorate-General 'Internal Market and Financial Services' (DG XV)
John Mogg, Thierry Stoll, John Farnell, Alexandros Spachis

Directorate-General 'Economic and Financial Affairs' (DG II)
Giovanni Ravasio, Jan Schmidt, Pierre Buigues

Directorate-General 'Industry' (DG III)
Stefano Micossi, Michel Ayral, Peter Smith

The studies were conducted by independent consultants (see the Single Market Review Series in Appendix C).

Appendix B

Results of Eurostat Business Survey

OPINION OF EUROPEAN ENTERPRISES ON THE IMPACT OF THE SINGLE MARKET PROGRAMME

Some 13,500 enterprises answered a survey conducted during the first half of 1995. The survey was designed to find out their opinions on the various types of measures adopted in implementing the single market and their impact on sales, competition and firms' strategies.

For 60 per cent of industrial enterprises, the elimination of customs formalities and border delays have had a beneficial effect on their activities. The deregulation of freight transport has been positive for less than half of the firms. The measures linked to the abolition of internal customs frontiers thus seem to have had a substantially positive effect for manufacturers. The measures aimed at eliminating technical barriers (the first four categories shown in Table 1 below), particularly those on the harmonisation of technical regulations and the mutual recognition of standards, have also had a globally positive net impact (net effect = positive effect – negative effect). The transitional arrangements for VAT, on the other hand, seem to have created some problems for enterprises, and almost 15 per cent of them noted negative effects from the changes in VAT procedures for intra-Community trade. Similarly, few enterprises have benefited from the opening of public procurement to competitive bidding, probably owing to the small number of firms concerned and the delays which have accumulated in the implementation of measures.

149

Type of measure	Percentage of enterprises reporting the effect of the European single market as:				Percentage of enterprises, weighted by the number of employees, reporting the effect of the European single market as:			
	Positive	No effect	Negative	No opinion	Positive	No effect	Negative	No opinion
Harmonisation of technical regulations and/or standards	31	51	9	9	40	45	8	8
Mutual recognition of technical regulations and/or standards	32	49	7	12	40	45	5	10
Conformity assessment procedures	23	56	5	15	27	55	4	13
Simplified patenting procedures	13	64	2	21	24	57	1	18
The opening up of public procurement	9	71	4	16	13	68	5	13
The elimination of customs documentation	60	30	5	5	69	23	5	3
Deregulation of freight transport	43	43	3	12	50	38	2	10
The elimination of delays at frontiers	56	35	2	7	63	31	1	5
The change in VAT procedures for intra EU sales	32	41	15	11	32	37	21	11
The liberalisation of capital movements	23	61	2	14	29	58	1	12
Double-taxation agreements	17	60	2	21	25	55	1	19

Table 1 Industrial enterprises

Source: Eurostat

It will be noted that a significant percentage of enterprises feel that the various types of Single Market measure have had no effect, or have no opinion. This is scarcely surprising, given the scope of the survey and the very specific nature of many of the measures.

Enterprises in the services sectors (excluding distributive trades), more of whose international trade takes place via foreign outlets, acknowledged at the time of the survey that they had been less directly affected by the single market. Some services sector industries, such as the hotel and restaurant trade, and real estate, have a large number of small enterprises which generally operate on the local or domestic market. In addition, certain directives, particularly those on insurance, had only recently been implemented at the time of the survey and had not had the time to produce any significant effect.

Despite this, the single market measures have had a widely positive effect on enterprises affected by the abolition of frontiers (see Table 2). In particular, the measures aimed at facilitating cross-border trade and deregulating movements of capital have had a substantially positive effect.

The percentage of enterprises in the services sector feeling that the Single Market has had no impact or having no opinion is higher than in manufacturing.

Type of measure	Percentage of enterprises reporting the effect of the European single market as:				Percentage of enterprises, weighted by the number of employees, reporting the effect of the European single market as:			
	Positive	No effect	Negative	No opinion	Positive	No effect	Negative	No opinion
Harmonisation of licensing/authorisation requirements	11	70	7	12	20	66	5	9
Mutual recognition of licences/authorisations	12	72	4	12	17	71	3	9
Measures to facilitate cross border operations	22	65	3	10	30	60	4	6
Measures to facilitate physical establishment in other EU states	9	78	1	12	17	74	1	8
The opening up of public procurement	9	73	4	15	16	68	6	9
The liberalisation of capital movements	16	72	1	10	25	66	1	8
Double taxation agreements	11	69	2	18	18	67	1	14

Table 2 Services enterprises (excluding distributive trades)

Source: Eurostat

These results are confirmed by the overall opinions (see Table 3) expressed by enterprises as a general assessment of the single market. Only 2 industrial enterprises in 10 felt that the single market had not achieved its principal objective, that is, eliminating the barriers to intra-Community trade. Manufacturing enterprises, and *a fortiori* those in the services sector, nevertheless agreed that it was too early yet to be talking of a genuine single market, and that further measures were needed.

Percentage of enterprises agreeing or disagreeing with the following statements on the single market						
Statement	Industry			Services (excluding distributive trades)		
	Agree	No opinion	Dis-agree	Agree	No opinion	Dis-agree
The single market programme has been successful in eliminating obstacles to EU trade in your sector	41	39	20	22	65	13
The single market programme has been successful in creating a genuine internal market in your sector	23	43	35	6	67	26
Additional measures are needed to eliminate obstacles to EU trade	27	61	12	18	75	7
Additional measures are needed in this sector to create a genuine internal market	25	61	14	17	76	7
The single market programme has been a success for your firm	33	40	27	16	63	21
The single market programme has been a success for your sector in your country	25	44	31	16	62	22
The single market programme has been a success for your sector in the European Union	29	51	20	15	71	14

Table 3 General opinions on the single market programme
Source: Eurostat

One of the aims of eliminating the barriers to trade was to promote greater competition on the market. In the industrial sector, it is the increase in the number of competitors from other Member States which is most keenly felt (see Table 4). As far as price competition is concerned, almost one firm in two recognises that it has met stiffer competition from other domestic firms or from those elsewhere in the Community. In the services sector the competition is essentially domestic. Competition from non-European enterprises is generally less perceptible.

Percentage of enterprises feeling that in recent years the level of competition has						
Statement	Manufacturing			Services (excluding distributive trades)		
	increased	stayed the same	decreased	increased	stayed the same	decreased
Number of competitors						
Domestically owned enterprises	25	64	11	30	63	7
Other EU owned enterprises	39	59	2	21	77	2
Non-EU owned enterprises	25	74	2	9	88	2
Price competition						
Domestically owned enterprises	44	51	4	37	60	3
Other EU owned enterprises	41	55	4	16	81	3
Non-EU owned enterprises	29	67	4	9	87	3
Product competition						
Domestically owned enterprises	33	64	3	27	69	4
Other EU owned enterprises	29	69	2	14	83	3
Non-EU owned enterprises	18	79	3	8	89	3

Table 4 Opinions on the trend in the level of competition

Source: Eurostat

If we look at the impact of the single market on sales in the manufacturing sector, it can be seen that around 3 enterprises in 10 recognise that the single market has stimulated their sales in other Member States. It is the medium-sized enterprises in the manufacturing sector, as well as the major corporations, which have benefited in particular from this growth.

Percentage of enterprises aware of an impact of the single market on their intra-Community sales								
	Manufacturing sectors				Services sector (excluding distributive trades)			
Number of persons employed in enterprise	Positive impact	No impact	Negative impact	Don't know	Positive impact	No impact	Negative impact	Don't know
20 – 49 (manufacturing) 5 – 49 (services)	25	63	4	7	12	76	2	9
50 – 199	32	58	4	6	16	76	1	6
200 – 499	34	58	4	4	16	78	0	6
500 – 999	27	63	7	3	19	73	1	7
More than 1,000	33	59	3	4	25	69	1	4
Total	28	61	4	6	12	76	2	9

Table 5 Opinion of enterprises on the impact of the single market on their sales in the EU

Source: Eurostat

More detailed sectoral analysis of the impact of the single market (see Table 6) reveals that not all markets have the same degree of openness to foreign trade, and that some enterprises have benefited more directly from measures of a more specifically sectoral nature. The high-technology sectors, such as electrical and electronic machinery and equipment, and those such as food, beverages and tobacco which have benefited from very specific measures, have a relatively positive perception of the single market. Those, on the other hand, which traditionally operate on a domestic basis, such as construction, hotels and restaurants, and the enterprise services and real estate sectors, have no strong views on the matter.

Percentage of enterprises agreeing or disagreeing with the statement that the single market has been a success for their sector in the EU							
Sector[1]	Agree	No opinion	Disagree	Sector	Agree	No opinion	Disagree
Food, beverages & tobacco (DA)	30	51	19	Transport equipment (DM)	25	59	16
Textiles, leather & furniture (DB+DC+DN)	31	47	22	Construction (F)	13	60	27
Wood, paper & printing/publishing (DD+DE)	19	59	22	Distributive trades (G)	16	68	15
Chemicals, rubber & plastics (DG+DH)	27	52	20	Hotels & restaurants (H)	15	75	10
Non-metallic mineral products (DI)	30	56	14	Transport, storage & communication (I)	21	60	19
Metal & metal products (DJ)	24	57	19	Financial intermediation (J)	27	57	17
Machinery & equipment (DK)	32	45	23	Real estate, renting & business activities (K)	10	75	15
Electrical & optical machinery (DL)	41	40	19				

Table 6 Opinions of the various sectors of activity

Source: Eurostat

[1] letters in brackets refer to NACE Rev. 1

Size has a fairly significant influence on the opinions of both industrial and service enterprises in the majority of answers to the questions on the impact of the single market. The larger the enterprise, the more likely it is to have transnational dealings and the more favourable its opinion of these measures (see Table 7). Small enterprises, on the other hand, tend to operate more on a regional or national basis, and seem to have been more aware of competition on their markets, with a consequently less enthusiastic view of the single market's success.

Percentage of enterprises agreeing or disagreeing with the statement that the single market programme has been a success for their company								
	Manufacturing				Services sector (excluding distributive trades)			
Number employed by the enterprise	Agree	No opinion	Disagree	Weight (1)	Agree	No opinion	Disagree	Weight (1)
20 – 49 (manufacturing) 5 – 49 (services)	30	42	28	60	16	63	21	91.9
50 – 199	36	37	27	30	18	61	21	5.8
200 – 499	40	35	25	7	17	61	22	1.5
500 – 999	38	38	24	2	21	54	25	0.5
More than 1,000	46	31	23	1	35	46	19	0.3
Total	33	40	27	100	16	63	21	100.0

(1) Proportion of enterprises in each class in the European total

Table 7 Effect of size on answers

Source: Eurostat

Finally, analysis of the impact by Member State shows that Member States' opinions vary widely (Table 8). Generally the single market has been more profitable to enterprises in the outlying Member States (in particular Greece and Ireland) and to those in Italy and Germany.

Percentage of enterprises agreeing or disagreeing with the statement that the single market programme has been a success for their company								
	Manufacturing				Services (excluding distributive trades)			
Member State	Agree	No opinion	Disagree	Weight % [1]	Agree	No opinion	Disagree	Weight % [1]
Belgie/Belgique	13	66	22	2	13	76	10	4
Danmark	33	41	27	2	27	54	20	2
BR Deutschland	41	40	18	20	NA [2]	NA [2]	NA [2]	NA [2]
Ellada	42	39	19	1	49	46	5	2
España	38	23	40	10	26	31	43	13
France	20	41	38	16	8	61	31	14
Ireland	46	38	15	1	22	64	14	1
Italia	54	23	23	22	45	38	17	11
Luxembourg	21	42	37	0	35	51	14	0
Nederland	17	64	19	4	6	72	23	8
Portugal	12	54	34	6	1	54	44	1
United Kingdom	16	59	25	16	9	79	12	41
Total	33	40	27	100	16	63	21	100

(1) Proportion of enterprises in each class in the European total.
(2) Not available. See 'Scope of the survey' in Methodology.

Table 8 National variations in opinions

Source: Eurostat

METHODOLOGY

The survey on the single market was carried out in 1995 on a sample of approximately 24,000 randomly selected enterprises representative of the European Union's production structure in terms of sector of activity, size and Member State of residence. The survey was carried out by mail and the response rate was approximately 56 per cent, representing a usable sample of about 13,500 enterprises. An additional small-scale telephone survey of non-respondents in Germany revealed that, on the whole, the opinions of non-respondents were very similar to those of respondents. Data were processed by Eurostat and weighted to reflect the structure of the population of European enterprises.

The operation was coordinated by Eurostat, and data collection was carried out by the following bodies: INS* (Belgium), Statistics Denmark*, IFO (Germany), National Statistical Service of Greece*, Ministry of Industry and Energy (Spain), ESRI in cooperation with the CSO* (Ireland), ISTAT* (Italy), INSEE* (France), NEI in cooperation with Statistics Netherlands*, INE* (Portugal), the NSO* (United Kingdom), Statec* (Luxembourg). It was financed by the European Commission.

Scope of the survey : all enterprises employing more than 20 persons in manufacturing and more than 5 persons in services.

In manufacturing, all activities are covered except the extractive industries and water and electricity production, ie Section D of NACE Rev. 1. The sector identified as 'distributive trades' corresponds to wholesale and retail trade and repair of motor vehicles and household goods, ie section G of NACE Rev. 1. The sector identified as 'services excluding distributive trades' corresponds to hotels and restaurants, transport and communications, financial intermediation, real estate, leasing and enterprise services, ie Sections H to K of NACE Rev. 1. It should be noted that enterprises in the construction industry (Section F of Nace Rev. 1) in Greece and in services excluding distributive trades in Germany could not be surveyed. Such enterprises are therefore not represented in the European averages given above.

The questionnaire: comprised 61 questions for manufacturing enterprises and 44 questions for service enterprises. In addition to the subjects discussed above, it also covered the impact on costs, productivity, profitability and employment, and enterprise strategy.

The percentages given in the tables are rounded off: it is therefore possible that the total of the percentages in a given row may be 99 per cent or 101 per cent owing to rounding errors.

For further information: a more detailed publication *Results of the Business Survey* forms part of the *Single Market Review* series (for a complete list of study titles, see Appendix C).

---

*National Statistical Institutes

Appendix C

The Single Market Review Series[1]

Subseries   **I – Impact on manufacturing**

Volume: 1   Food, drink and tobacco processing machinery ('Food & drink machinery') – *DRI Europe Ltd*

    2   Pharmaceutical products ('Pharmaceuticals') – *REMIT*

    3   Textiles and clothing ('Textiles') – *CEGOS SA*

    4   Construction site equipment ('Construction') – *W.S. Atkins*

    5   Chemicals ('Chemicals') – *KPMG*

    6   Motor vehicles ('Vehicles') – *Ernst & Young*

    7   Processed foodstuffs ('Foodstuffs') – *Bureau Européen de Recherches ('BER')*

    8   Telecommunications equipment ('Telecom. equipment') – *Analysys Ltd*

Subseries   **II – Impact on services**

Volume: 1   Insurance ('Insurance') – *CEGOS SA*

    2   Air transport ('Air transport') – *Cranfield University*

    3   Credit institutions and banking ('Banking') – *Economic Research Europe Ltd*

    4   Distribution ('Distribution') – *Coopers & Lybrand*

    5   Road freight transport ('Road freight') – *NEA*

    6   Telecommunications: liberalized services ('Telecom. services') – *Bossard Consultants SA*

    7   Advertising ('Advertising') – *Bocconi University*

    8   Audio-visual services and production ('Audio-visual') – *KPMG*

9   Single information market ('Information') – *Analysys Ltd*
10   Single energy market ('Energy') – *London Economies*
11   Transport networks ('Transport') – *Trasporti e Territorio*

Subseries   **III – Dismantling of barriers**
Volume: 1   Technical barriers to trade ('Technical barriers') – *W.S. Atkins*

2   Public procurement ('Procurement') – *Eurostrategy Consultants*

3   Customs and fiscal formalities at frontiers ('Customs & frontiers') – *Price Waterhouse*

4   Industrial property rights ('Industrial property') – *CJA Consultants Ltd*

5   Capital market liberalization ('Capital markets') – *National Institute for Economic & Social Research (NIESR)*

6   Currency management costs ('Currency costs') – *IFO-Institut*

Subseries   **IV – Impact on trade and investment**
Volume: 1   Foreign direct investment ('FDI') – *Economists Advisory Group Ltd ('EAG')*

2   Trade patterns inside the single market ('Trade patterns') – *CEPII*

3   Trade creation and trade diversion ('Trade creation/diversion') – *Centre for Economic Policy Research (CEPR)*

4   External access to European markets ('External access') – *University of Sussex & Southbank University*

Subseries   **V – Impact on competition and scale effects**
Volume: 1   Price competition and price convergence ('Price convergence') – *DRI Europe Ltd*

2   Intangible investments ('Intangibles') – *RCS Conseil*

3   Competition issues ('Competition') – *London Economics*

4   Economies of scale ('Scale economies') – *Economists Advisory Group Ltd ('EAG')*

Subseries	**VI – Aggregate and regional impact**
Volume: 1	Regional growth and convergence ('Regional growth') – *Cambridge Econometrics*
2	The cases of Greece, Spain, Ireland and Portugal ('Greece, Spain, Ireland & Portugal') – *ESRI*
3	Trade, labour and capital flows: the less developed regions ('Trade & capital flows') – *CERES*
4	Employment, trade and labour costs in manufacturing ('Employment & manufacturing') – *Cambridge Econometrics*
5	Aggregate results of the single market programme ('Aggregate results') – *National Technical University of Athens*

Note

1   38 studies co-published by Kogan Page and the Office for Official Publications of the European Communities

Results of the business survey ('Business survey') – *Eurostat*

SINGLE MARKET REVIEW

In January 1997 Kogan Page, on behalf of the European Commission, will commence publication of the long-awaited 39 volume *Single Market Review*, the first authoritative picture of the effect of economic union on European industry and its competitiveness.

These volumes provide a detailed overview of all aspects of the Single Market, giving essential information to all those, worldwide, who are interested or involved in its development, as well as an invaluable insight to specific industry sectors for investors, analysts and corporate strategists. Written by leading subject experts and co-ordinated by specialists from the Commission, there is no leader in British Industry who can afford to ignore them!

For *further information* on any of the following titles, or to place an order, please contact Emma Gilkes at Kogan Page on 44 (0) 171 278 0433 (tel) or 44 (0) 171 837 6348 (fax), quoting MON 1

- -

Please use this form in conjunction with your official purchase order or enclose your full ordering details including delivery address on a separate piece of paper.

Payment can be made in two ways. Please tick the appropriate box:

☐ I enclose a cheque (made payable to Kogan Page) for £ ....
☐ I authorise you to debit my credit card account for £ ....

My Access/Visa/Amex/Diner's Card number is:

| | | | | | | | | | | | | | | | | | | | | | |

Expiry date: ....

Card Holder's name: ....

Address: ....

....

 Kogan Page Ltd., 120 Pentonville Road, London, N1 9JN, England

A complete set of all 39 volumes	£1650

Series I: Impact on Manufacturing

Food, Drink and Tobacco
Processing Industry
   DRI Europe Ltd.   £40

Pharmaceutical Products
   REMIT Consultants   £40

Textiles and Clothing
   CEGOS SA   £45

Construction Site Equipment
   W.S. Atkins / IFO   £40

Chemicals
   KPMG   £45

Motor Vehicles
   Ernst & Young   £50

Processed foodstuffs
   BER with Wye College   £50

Telecommunications Equipment
   Analysys   £40

Series II: Impact on Services

Insurance
   CEGOS   £40

Air Transport
   Cranfield University   £45

Credit Institutions and Banking
   Economic Research Europe   £55

Distribution
   Coopers & Lybrand   £45

Road Freight Transport
   NEA & CERT   £40

Telecommunications: Liberalized
services
   Bossard Consultants   £40

Advertising
   Bocconi University   £40

Audio-Visual Services and
Production
   KPMG   £40

Single Information Market
   Analysys Ltd.   £40

Single Energy Market
   London School of Economics   £45

Transport Networks
   AT Kearney   £40

Series III: Dismantling of Barriers

Technical Barriers to Trade
   W.S. Atkins   £45

Public Procurement
   Eurostrategy Consultants   £50

Customs and Fiscal Formalities at
Frontiers
   Price Waterhouse   £45

Industrial Property Rights
   CJA Consultants   £40

Capital Market Liberalization
   NIESR   £40

Currency Management Costs
   IFO-Institut   £55

Series IV: Impact on Trade and Investment

Foreign Direct Investment
   Economics Advisory Group Ltd.   £50

Trade Patterns inside the Single
Market
   CEPII & CIREM with FIES   £45

Trade Creation and Trade
Diversion
   CEPR   £45

External Access to European
Markets
   University of Sussex   £45

Series V: Impact on Competition and Scale Effects

Price Competition and Price
Convergence
   DRI Consultants   £45

Intangible Investments
   RCS Conseil   £45

Competition Issues
   London School of Economics   £55

Economies of Scale
   Economists Advisory Group Ltd.   £45

Series VI: Aggregate and Regional Impact

Regional Growth and Convergence
   Cambridge Econometrics   £40

The Cases of Greece, Spain,
Ireland and Portugal
   ESRI   £50

Trade, Labour and Capital Flows:
The Less Developed Regions
   CERES   £55

Employment and Labour Costs in
Manufacturing
   Cambridge Econometrics   £50

Aggregate Results of the Single
Market Programme (Two Studies)
   Technical University of Athens   £40

Results of the Business Survey

   Eurostat   £45